Systems Analysis
in Libraries

SYSTEMS ANALYSIS
in Libraries

a question and answer approach

CHET GOUGH
&
TAVEREKERE SRIKANTAIAH

LINNET BOOKS CLIVE BINGLEY

HAMDEN • CT   LONDON

©Chester R. Gough and Taverekere Srikantaiah 1978
First published in 1978 in the United States of America
as a Linnet Book, an imprint of The Shoe String Press, Inc.,
Hamden, Connecticut
and simultaneously published in the United Kingdom
by Clive Bingley, Ltd,
London
Printed in the United States of America

Library of Congress Cataloging in Publication Data

Gough, Chet.
  Systems analysis in libraries.

  Bibliography: p.
  Includes index.
  1. Library administration. 2. System analysis. 3. Libraries—Automation. I Srikantaiah, Taverekere, joint author. II Title.
Z678.G676 1978   025.1   78-7539
ISBN 0-208-01753-4

[Linnet] ISBN 0-208-01753-4
[Bingley] ISBN 0 85157 278 2

Contents

Preface

This guide grew out of the need for a concise aid for students in the course on systems analysis in libraries. The course, offered in the Division of Library Science, California State University, Fullerton, rested on extensive readings and exercises. The purpose of the guide was to synthesize the common elements in a variety of sources and to serve as the unifying theme of the course.

In a field as active as systems analysis, it becomes necessary to choose between being concise and being comprehensive. For the purposes of this guide, the choice was to be concise. The sources cited in the bibliography reflect the scope and variety of the field without attempting to be exhaustive or complete, while the text remains a manageable length. It seemed better to give the student a framework on which to build according to his needs than to attempt an exhaustive treatment of the field. In our own course, the guide did provide this framework; we believe it may serve other instructors and students in the same way.

We wish to express our thanks to those students whose energy and enthusiasm contributed greatly to our courses and whose comments and questions aided us in developing the guide. A special note of appreciation goes as well to Susan Sim who typed the first version of the text. While it is not possible to identify all of the influences which contributed to this work, we wish to acknowledge the intensive use of the works of Robinson, Cougar, and Buckland. We are, of course, responsible for the form and content of the text as it now stands.

Library Systems Analyst, OCLC, Inc.,   Chet Gough
Columbus, Ohio

Documentation Systems Analyst,   Taverekere Srikantaiah
World Bank, Washington, D.C.

Systems Analysis
in Libraries

Introduction

The literature of systems and systems analysis has become so extensive in the last decade that it becomes difficult for the novice to find his way among the subtle variations introduced by different disciplinary approaches to the subject. The purpose of this work is to select the most important topics of systems analysis, present these topics as succinctly as possible, and provide a guide through the literature by means of selected references. Ten chapters are organized to show the progression of a systems study, beginning with the definition of the system and ending with the evaluation of systems.

Within each of the chapters, the key concepts are examined by a combination of narrative text and a series of questions and answers. The text provides an introduction to terminology in context so that terms become familiar as one progresses through the tracts. The questions and answers anticipate those elements of systems study which cause difficulty for those beginning an investigation of system analysis. At the end of each chapter, a selected list of references provides the sources which extend the material in the body of the tract. By reading the text and the references provided, it is possible to build logically from general concepts and theories to the application of techniques.

A series of exercises is included to provide experience with the techniques. These are relatively simple exercises intended to reinforce the description and to provide an opportunity to verify one's ability to work with the methods. The exercises are limited to those for which useful exercises can be designed.

1. Understanding systems

What would it mean to you if you could find a way to arrange all the elements of your life so that you could clearly identify what it is that you want from life, determine the ways in which you might obtain it, and have a continuing means of evaluating your accomplishments? This is the ideal which systems analysis offers for organizations in general and for libraries in particular.

We do not achieve ideals in most instances; we are only able to reach approximations. The ideal, however, provides a standard against which we measure what has been done. Systems analysis is a combination of conceptual and analytical tools which give us the capacity to identify ideals and to measure the degree to which we achieve them. Since change is an integral part of our real world as well as our ideal world, there is a continuing cycle. The ideal is determined, action is taken to achieve it, and the results are evaluated. From the evaluation, we may modify our ideal, change our actions or change both ideal and action, and repeat the cycle. This reiterative process is characteristic of systems analysis and the systems approach. It becomes important to remember, however, that the notion of a system is an abstraction; the reality is the work accomplished in an organization, or, in systems terms, the transformations of material completed in the system. To enlarge on this idea, we begin by examining the concept of a system.

What is a system?

A system is everything and nothing. The notion of a system is a hypothetical construct, a form of abstraction we use to identify patterns in the empirical world around us. The notion rests on a series of assumptions. To gain some understanding of these assumptions, we must begin with Bertalanffy's general systems theory, for this is the source of many of our basic concepts.

Bertalanffy's purpose in general systems theory is to present arguments to show that general systems theory provides a more powerful paradigm for scientific investigation than the present formulation of the scientific method. His definitions reflect his concern for generalizing the scientific method in ways which will accommodate problems involving multiple variables. While the notion of a system is derived from many different areas of science, it is always perceived as an entity "consisting of interacting parts." (32:19)*

The interaction must be complex, in the mathematical sense of dynamic rather than linear, so that elements of the system are not necessarily additive. In the several sections of *General Systems Theory,* Bertalanffy treats the concept of a system from a thermodynamic perspective (32:34), mathematically by distinguishing between summative and constitutive relationships (32:54f), as "open systems" actively tending toward increased organization (32:150), and as a machine with input (32:97). These theoretical formulations lead to much more general problems of scientific method than we need to consider here. Our purpose is to apply the systems

---

* References indicate the number of the item in the Bibliography and the page in the item.

approach and the resulting techniques to library operations and problems. For our purposes, other investigators provide more useful definitions.

While variations occur among these investigators, they reiterate the same meaning, for example:

> Although . . . the word "system" has been defined in many ways, all definers agree that a system is a set of parts coordinated to accomplish a set of goals. (86:29)

> A system is a collection of interrelated parts which is unified by a design to obtain one or more objectives. (214:1)

> We will define a system as an array of components designed to accomplish a particular objective according to plan. (173:5)

These definitions emphasize the interrelatedness of the parts of a system. However, we need to extend our concept of a system. Churchman, presenting the view of the management scientist, indicates a need to keep the following five points in mind:

1. The total system objectives and, more specifically, the performance measures of the whole system;
2. The system environment; the fixed constraints;
3. The resources of the system;
4. The components of the system, their activities, goals and measures of performance;
5. The management of the system. (86:29)

Luchsinger, speaking more directly from the point of view of the systems analyst, also adds five qualifying elements or "implications":
1. A system must be designed to accomplish an objective.
2. The elements of a system must have an established arrangement.
3. Interrelationships must exist among the individual

elements of a system, and these interrelationships must be synergistic in nature.

4. The basic ingredients of a process (the flow of information, energy, and materials) are more vital than the basic elements of the system.

5. Organization objectives are more important than the objectives of its elements, and thus, there is a deemphasis of the parochial objectives of the elements of a system. (214:1)

These definitions and their qualifiers view the system from inside. In order to gain a comprehensive view, we need to consider systems from the outside. The basic model of a system is one in which inputs are taken from the environment, transformed in some way into outputs which are put back into the environment. This process of exchange distinguishes open systems from closed systems and is characteristic of biological and social systems. It is the notion of open systems which combine interrelated parts and interact with their environment that makes the systems approach such a powerful analytical tool.

What principles of general systems theory contribute to its value for the study of any system?

The first [principle] is the principle of equifinality. In any closed system, the final state is unequivocally determined by the initial conditions: e.g. the motion in a planetary system where the positions of the planets at a time t are unequivocally determined by their positions at time t_0. Or in a chemical equilibrium, the final concentration of the reactants naturally depends on the initial concentrations. If either the initial conditions or the process is altered, the final state will also be changed. This is not so in open systems. Here, the same final state may be reached from different initial conditions and in different ways. . . . (32:40)

In addition to equifinality, open systems share a number of

other characteristics which contribute to the power of the systems approach. They are characterized by a cycle of events, negative entropy, coding signals from the environment, and negative feedback. The events are the actions taken to transform inputs and are repeated over time in a continuing cycle. Negative entropy tends to increase organizational complexity and decrease disorder. The system uses coded signals from the environment to get information about its own performance. It enters the negative feedback loop and provides the data the system requires to make corrective adjustments. The corrective adjustments react to disruptive forces which may interfere with system functions so that a steady state is approximated through a process analogous to homeostasis. This provides a means of modifying variations in the system to achieve a balance among the several parts of the system. The fluctuations resulting from these corrective actions also lead to further differentiation and elaboration of specialized functions which in turn contribute still further to the increase in negative entropy.

Entropy is an elementary force in nature. Bertalanffy discusses the notion of negative entropy.

Another apparent contrast between inanimate and animate nature is what sometimes was called the violent contradiction between Lord Kelvin's degradation and Darwin's evolution, between the law of dissipation in physics and the law of evolution in biology. According to the second principle of thermodynamics, the general trend of events in physical nature is toward states of maximum disorder and levelling down of differences, with the so-called heat death of the universe as the final outlook, when all energy is degraded into evenly distributed heat of low temperature, and the world process comes to a stop. In contrast, the living world shows, in embryonic development and in evolution, a transition towards higher order, heterogeneity, and organization. . . . Thus living systems, maintaining themselves in a steady state, can avoid the increase of entropy and may even develop towards states of increased order and organization. (32:41)

Thus, the general nature of these characteristics of open systems give the systems approach two very important sources of power as an analytical method: it offers three levels of analysis through systems theory, systems management, and systems analysis; and it provides a means of identifying a system at many different levels—social institutions, organizations, and parts of organizations. The conceptual model of systems theory is expanded into a pragmatic means of designing and operating organizations in systems management and elaborated into systems analysis which provides a powerful methodology for solving problems within organizations.

The concepts presented thus far can be summarized in a brief statement of the principles of general systems theory:

1. *The Principle of Equifinality.* Open systems arrive at a final state or condition through variations in process and variations in initial states or conditions and may still reach defined goals, objectives or purposes.
2. *The Principle of Information.* Open systems operate by means of information which is used as a medium of interaction among the elements of the system. Some of this information is used in feedback loops within the system to maintain control of the system.
3. *The Principle of Organization.* Open systems function in ways which are contrary to some physical systems by tending toward increased organization (or negative entropy) rather than toward disorganization and this action results from a favorable balance in the exchange of energy and information between the system and the environment.
4. *The Principle of Teleology.* Open systems demonstrate characteristics of purposiveness and tend toward defined objectives which may vary according to particular states of the system in time and use processes of differentiation, growth, feedback and organization to move toward these objectives.

The principles still treat systems and their characteristics as abstractions. While we can begin to see the characteristics of systems, it is necessary to examine these characteristics in terms of the organizations in which we carry on the functions of our society. To take this next step, we consider a third question.

*What are some of the characteristics
of social organizations that make them open systems?*

Katz and Kahn (177) provide us with a summary of the characteristics of open systems. In the list which follows, "open system" becomes synonomous with "social organization."

1. Importation of energy. Open systems import some form of energy from the external environment. . . . No social structure is self-sufficient or self-contained.
2. The throughput. Open systems transform the energy available to them. . . . Some work gets done in the system.
3. The output. Open systems export some product into the environment, whether it be the invention of an inquiring mind or a bridge constructed by an engineering firm.
4. Systems as cycle of events. The pattern of activities in the energy exchange has a cyclic character. The product exported into the environment furnishes the sources of energy for the repetition of the cycle of activities.
5. Negative entropy. To survive, open systems must move to arrest the entropic process; they must acquire negative entropy. The entropic process is a universal law of nature in which all forms of organization move toward disorganization or death. . . . There is then a general trend in an open system to maximize its ratio of imported to expended energy, to survive and even during periods of crisis to live on borrowed time. . . .
6. Information input, negative feedback, and the coding process. The inputs into living systems consist not

only of energic materials which become transformed or altered in the work that gets done. Inputs are also informative in character and furnish signals to the structure about the environment and about its own functioning in relation to the environment. . . .
8. Differentiation. Open systems move in the direction of differentiation and elaboration. Diffuse global patterns are replaced by more specialized functions.
9. Equifinality. Open systems are further characterized by the principle of equifinality, a principle suggested by von Bertalanffy in 1940. According to this principle, a system can reach the same final state from different initial conditions and by a variety of paths. . . . (177:14–29)

The nature of open systems allows us to define a particular system as a unit in an organization, an organization, a social institution, or a society. In each case, the object of study is in direct and dynamic relationship with its environment. We can see, then, that:

A system is an organized or complex whole; an assemblage or combination of things or parts forming a complex whole. But each unitary whole, as described, must maintain some relationship with other systems. That is, each receives inputs and, after a transformation of some kind takes place, each produces output that will be input for other systems. Therein lies the basic concept of systems theory: the input, transformation, and output model. Once this general framework is established, the interesting task is to determine how these associations can be arranged, and how the transformation process of each contributes to the whole. It is a philosophical and conceptual way of thinking, a way of establishing hierarchies of relationships, a way of associating activities with other activities so that relationships can be identified and classified properly. (174:503)

The generality of the systems approach provides a very

powerful way of approaching problems. Once we have perceived the conceptual framework, we can apply it to a wide range of situations from the elemental units of society, such as marriage or family, to the major institutions, such as the systems of justice, economics, education, or government. This is the beginning from which we can build our models and our analytical tools. With these tools, we can begin to approximate our ideal system. The analytical processes will be relatively straightforward. It is in our cultural attitudes and our belief systems that we will encounter the major obstacles to applying sound systems analysis to our existing institutions.

Selected Readings

An * indicates preferred readings.

*Ackoff, Russell L. 1971. Towards a system of systems concepts. *Management Science* 17:661–671.
Also in *Systems analysis techniques,* ed. J. Daniel Couger and R.W. Knapp, pp. 27–38. New York: Wiley.
Bertalanffy, L. Von. 1968. *General systems theory: Foundations, Development, and Applications.* New York: George Braziller.
*Bertalanffy, L. Von. 1972. The history and status of general systems theory. In *Trends in general systems theory,* ed. G. J. Klir, pp. 21–38. New York: Wiley.
Also in Couger and Knapp, pp. 9–26.
Churchman, C. West. 1968. *The systems approach.* 1–78. New York: Delta.
Johnson, Richard A., Newell, William T. and Vergin, Robert C. 1972. The systems approach—an integrative philosophy. In *Operations management: a systems concept,* pp. 501–17. New York: Houghton Mifflin.
*Katz, Daniel, and Kahn, R. L. 1966. Organizations and the systems concept. In *The social psychology of organizations,* pp. 14–29. New York: Wiley.

2. The library as a system

The library is a social organization. As such, it demonstrates the characteristics of open systems: input, transformation, output, a cycle of events, negative entropy, feedback, dynamic homeostasis, and equifinality. We must be careful, however, to distinguish the librarian's terminology from systems terminology. When librarians speak of information, they often mean books, journals, films, or other materials. This is not always the sense intended when the systems analyst speaks of information. It will be useful, then, to examine the characteristics of open systems in relation to the library as a system.

We will use the characteristics of open systems identified by Katz and Kahn (177:14–29) for our model. By proceeding through each of these characteristics, it will be possible to match open system characteristics with characteristics of the library and also to indicate when terms are used in particular ways.

The importation of energy is relatively clear. The library obtains staff and funds from its environment and both are forms of energy or are converted to energy and materials. The throughput and output of the library may be less obvious. Certainly, some work gets done in the system, but what is the throughput and output? The library actually creates something which did not previously exist when it performs its transformation. Books and other "knowledge packages" are acquired by the library. The transformation occurs when the staff, using their energy, analyze the materials to create records which represent the materials, and label them in order to organize the library's collections. The true output of the library is the intangible process of relating the physical item—the book, recording, or film—to a concept or idea. This process is accomplished in two ways: by classifying items to integrate them into a set of items treating the same subject, and by describing them so that records representing the item can be displayed in the catalog according to different principles of arrangement. The result, of course, is a collection of materials arranged according to a classification scheme and a catalog providing a subject index to the same materials. Maintaining a collection of items which can be lent to members of the user community is another form of output; its value, however, depends on the organization of the items and the index (catalog) which aids in finding them.

It is not difficult to see the cycle of events in the library. New publications are added to the collection and old ones are removed. Publications are borrowed, returned, and borrowed again. In some instances, the publications are lent and transformed by authors into new publications which are added to the collection.

Negative entropy becomes much more difficult to identify. In one sense, the creation of the catalog can be considered a form of stored energy: it represents an energy investment and would require large quantities of energy to replace. Entropy is a process, however, and, therefore, negative entropy must also be a process. The former tends toward disorder and the latter tends toward order. In this sense, negative entropy becomes the accumulated knowledge (experience) of the staff as they continue to learn about operating the library and work to improve it. Negative entropy is related to information, input, feedback, and the coding process.

Information input is clear. The library gets two kinds of information from its environment: information about new publications and information about its operation. The first type of information provides the library with messages about items to be acquired. The output from the knowledge industry becomes input for the library. The second type of information provides messages about the way the library achieves its goals. This information concerning the library's operations is feedback.

The use of the term "negative feedback" is unfortunate, for the notion of feedback is a simple one. It stems from Norbert Wiener's work on cybernetics (328) and means information derived from a process which is fed back into the process in order to control the system. Feedback is neither "negative" nor "positive"; it is neutral. The change that feedback may induce depends on the state of the process when the feedback is received. Normally, feedback comes to the library in the form of complaints or of praise. We are apt to accept praise uncritically but we always examine complaints critically. Were we to examine both in the same way, it is probable that some praise would be received with satisfaction while some might be used to initiate changes. Similarly, complaints often indicate a failure in the system and we analyze them to see whether or not changes might be initiated to correct the problem that generated the complaint. In both cases, the library receives information from its environment, and this information, when used advantageously, contributes to improvements in the system. This is a form of negative entropy which tends to increase order within the system. The coding process is a part of this information exchange, but may be less direct than the other two.

Complaints about material in the collection, for example, are a form of feedback. They must be evaluated with the same care as other messages, but they may also indicate changes in the user community. This could mean that some changes are needed in the library in order to meet the needs of the community. The difficulty with coded messages is the ambiguity they demonstrate, and the consequent difficulty in interpreting them. Complaints about materials might prompt the library to investigate further to see whether this is typical of the entire community or an of an isolated part. Such complaints might also be used to initiate action by the library to identify and encourage support from those who consider the freedom to read fundamental in the society.

Complaints about materials occasionally become a disruptive force, some communities have experienced severe crises as a result of such complaints. The consequence will often be an intensive examination of the purposes and goals of the library and may have serious effects on the library. Over time, with careful effort, the equilibrium will be restored, but the library will not be exactly the same as it was in its previous state. A budget crisis will have a similar impact, and the energy of the library may be diverted to greater public relations efforts and to more careful justification of expenditures. These counteracting forces will prevent a true steady state from occurring, but they also work toward maintaining the system in a state of reasonable balance or homeostasis.

The most characteristic pattern in the western world has been growth. Growth leads to differentiation of functions and to specialization more rapidly than other factors might. It will be useful to keep this under surveillance as growth trends tend to flatten out in our society. In the library, differentiation is a result of growth and is evident in the division between reader services and technical services. The subdivision of reader services into subject units is another indication of differentiation and specialization. The tendency toward specialization characterized by the emergence of special libraries will be accelerated by the appearance of new forms of information services based on computers and telecommunications capabilities.

Finally, equifinality is apparent to any library user. Each library, to some extent, provides the same services and the same types of materials. Each, however, demonstrates idiosyncratic differences in the procedures, policies, and organizational climate of the library. The goal remains the same in its most general form, but the means differ in many ways from library to library.

The library is an open system in contemporary society. It

has all the characteristics of an open system and does exchange energy with its environment. As a social organization, however, the library can also be defined by its subsystems.

What are the subsystems of the library?

The library subsystems identified by Chapman (84:8) include: administration, reference, acquisitions, cataloging and classification, serials and circulation. This list is modified in the *Handbook of Data Processing for Libraries* (151:384), part four of which is devoted to analyzing library subsystems. Hayes adds two activities as subsystems: interlibrary loan and mechanized (i.e. commercial) information services. While all of these can be viewed as subsystems, there are alternative views. The serials system, for example, can be considered a component of the acquisitions system, while both interlibrary loan and mechanized information services may be components in the reference subsystem.

Of these identified subsystems, the provision of commercial information services is a projected service that has been tested in a limited way in public libraries and is offered as a regular service in some university and special libraries. The cost of the services and the methods of funding them are still in very tentative stages for public libraries. When they are incorporated into the public and university library services, they may fall into a specialized category as serials acquisition has, because of the differences in operations.

The serial record subsystem of the library differs sufficiently from the acquisition system for monographs to demand a separate analysis of its functions in order to develop efficient and effective files and procedures. The serial order process represents only a part of this subsystem while much more effort is directed to maintaining records, to processing incoming issues, or to claiming missing issues. Since medical libraries with the longest experience in providing mechanized information services have incorporated MEDLINE requests into the reference function, it is probable that such services will be provided in this way until the demand exceeds the capacity of the reference department. If the serials subsystem is considered a separate subsystem and judgment concerning the mechanized information services is reserved pending more experience, we consider the subsystems in the Chapman list as our operational guide to subsystems in the library.

The subsystems of the library interact at many different points. As an example, we can review the interaction between the cataloging and the reference systems as an example from library history. The recent developments with cataloging data networks and computer output on microfilm catalogs will modify this interaction in the future. Here, we consider the classical problem of cost trade-off.

The cataloging subsystem of the library is concerned with the problem of description and identification of items in the library's collection as well as the subject specification of those items. The descriptive function is performed by carrying out the procedures defined in the *Anglo American Cataloging Rules* (AACR) or by locating the cataloging data distributed by the Library of Congress and commercial vendors. The cataloging data is converted into the form adopted by the library for its catalog: cards, book catalogs, microform catalogs, or on-line catalogs.

The reference subsystem uses the output of the cataloging subsystem as a primary means of locating publications from which responses can be obtained to meet the user's needs. While the experience and skill of the person performing the reference function will effect the use of the catalog, the quality and responsiveness of the catalog will determine the efficiency with which it can be used.

With these two systems, we have a cataloging system with the goal of processing materials as efficiently as possible. This is often interpreted as use of the available catalog copy, the acceptance of standard subject heading lists, and conformity to the AACR. In contrast to this objective, the reference subsystem objectives are to respond as quickly as possible to the inquiry and to be able to identify the appropriate work with the least effort. The objective is often translated into a desire for subject headings more closely related to current usage of terms and subject headings reflecting new topics of interest.

The question can be reduced to terms of costs. The cataloging subsystem becomes more efficient—the least time and effort is required to process a title—when there is little or no modification of the cataloging data that can be retrieved from other sources. The reference subsystem becomes more efficient when additional subject headings are used, when new subject headings are included, or the syndetic apparatus is modified to reflect new terms or changes in the use of terms. The cost trade between more extensive cataloging to reduce reference costs or increased reference costs to reduce cataloging costs is a typical example of the dynamics of subsystem and system objectives.

The dilemma can be resolved only by moving to the system level to analyze the problem in relation to overall system objectives. When this is done, the search begins for alternatives which may or may not be immediately apparent. It becomes a direct search, however, to find ways in which cataloging and reference costs can be maintained at the lowest levels consistent with library objectives. In an ideal situation, the solution becomes synergistic and the efforts of the reference staff are joined to the efforts of the cataloging staff to create an overarching system with greater functional effectiveness.

While the cost trade-off between cataloging and reference is beginning to be less relevant with the development of new reference tools, it indicates the need for several levels of analysis to avoid the problem of improving one subsystem at the expense of another. The goal of the systems study is to develop methods of improving overall effectiveness rather than improving the efficiency of one component. This goal operates at many levels. We have considered the interaction between two subsystems within the library, but we get a different perspective when we look at the relationships between systems.

What distinguishes large-scale systems
from small-scale systems?

While there is a tendency to emphasize the origins of the

systems approach and systems analysis in operations research and studies of weapon systems carried out by the Department of Defense, systems analysis, as it is presently conceived, represents the convergence of two mainstreams of effort: the systems engineering approach noted above and the efforts of accountants, office managers, and data processing managers to find both descriptive methods and analytical techniques to study work situations involving information, data, and records.

Leimkuhler in his article "Large Scale Library Systems" (201:580) reflects on two aspects of these converging efforts: the growing awareness that the library is a subsystem in larger communications and social systems, and the need to address problems as they occur in the working situations of existing libraries. The problem at one end of the spectrum is reflected in the report of the National Commission on Libraries and Information Services which is developing public policy and determining the eventual shape of information services at the national level. At the other end of the spectrum, we have the examples of systems studies in individual libraries.

The conflict eventually reduces to the question of what action can be taken immediately to resolve the urgent problems of daily operations. As an example of the large-scale systems approach, *Limits to Growth,* published by the Club of Rome, used a computer model of the world's food supply to analyze the prospects for the future. The result was a dismal projection which required major decisions by 1975. These decisions apparently have not been made. The problem, however, is that the model simplified the factors relating to food supply and consumption to such an extent that the results of the projection become questionable. While the prediction of a critical point late in this century is probably accurate, the deficiencies in the model have generated widespread scepticism toward the report. The task of creating responsive models of large-scale systems that accurately reflect physical and social systems becomes extremely complex.

Leimkuhler identifies small-scale systems as those which

. . . are small because the work can be easily confined to limited areas of study, using well-tested methods, measuring a limited number of variables, employing self-evident measures of effectiveness, and causing little radical change to existing organizational structures. (201:580)

The implications of this dichotomy clearly place the library systems study within the realm of the possible. While even small-scale systems studies entail costs, the order of magnitude is such that they can often be accomplished with the existing staff and resources. Within this framework, then, we can consider the implications of systems study for the very small library.

What value does systems analysis have for the smaller library?

It is useful to distinguish again between the term "large-scale system" and the relative terms "large" and "small" as they relate to library size. As Leimkuhler points out, the distinction between large-scale and small-scale systems is one of scope. The large-scale approach implies a multi-organizational study of specific social, political, or information needs. Within the systems literature, it is true that considerable emphasis is directed to very large organizations, but it is not only the large organization that can benefit from systems work:

Large teams are not always needed to make use of systems analysis. It is poor judgment to develop a million dollar solution to a ten thousand dollar problem. While there are many governmental problems which warrant large scale analysis, there are even more problems where a relatively small effort can produce useful results. . . .

The systems approach can be viewed as a general process within which a wide variety of specific techniques may be employed depending on the particular problem under analysis. The systems analysis process can be used by almost any city, large or small, both to improve existing programs and to develop and institute new programs. . . . (223:2)

Systems analysis is appropriate for both large and small organizations. It must be recognized that the benefits to be realized will be related to the size of the organization and the scope of the study. This is, of course, reflected in lower costs for studies of smaller libraries. It is unlikely that the relationships between system study costs, system study benefits, and organizational size are linearly related over the full range of sizes of libraries. It is probably true, however, that the benefits of systems studies on smaller organizations may have greater impact on the organization's operations. Similarly, for the same kind of benefit, the system study itself becomes much less complex because of the reduction in the number of relationships (an exponential function) as well as the lower volume of transactions. This difference in scale between studies of large libraries and small libraries is reflected in the next question, which considers the way systems studies are conducted.

Is there a generalized methodology
for systems analysis of libraries?

The system study is conducted in ways that are very similar to the conduct of any form of inquiry. These methods have become sufficiently standard to be completely general; they apply to all types of operations regardless of the activities being performed by the organization. The important task of the analyst is to select from the array of techniques available those which will be most productive in the type and size of organization under study. The other point which must be kept in mind is that the steps in the system study are abstractions used to identify the purpose of each phase. In actual practice, the process is less clearly defined and often much more interactive. Some models presented in the literature serve as illustrations.

Hayes reduces the steps in the system study to five: define, analyze, synthesize, evaluate, reiterate the first four (151).

Fasana suggests six slightly different steps to accomplish the same end: preliminary study, descriptive phase, analysis phase, design and development phase, implementation phase, and evaluation and feedback phase. (121:472f).

Parker further extends these steps to eight: statement of needs, define objectives of the study, define the constraints, generate alternatives, analyze and select the best alternative, implement the selected alternative for testing, evaluate the experimental system, feedback results and modify the system until the objectives are met (223:4).

The many variations in the terms used and the intent of the step or phase of the study suggests the applicability of a generalized version of the standard research model as follows:

1. Definition of the Problem. State the problem to be solved, the scope of the study and the limitations imposed on the study.
2. Data Collection. Gather the relevant quantitative, qualitative, and descriptive information related to the objectives of the study, e.g., number of staff by grade, organizational structure, responsibilities, forms, processes, outputs, etc.
3. Analysis. Examine the data using the appropriate techniques for each type of data, e.g., procedures analysis, flow charting, forms analysis, etc.
4. Synthesis. Design new components or redesign existing components to achieve system objectives.
5. Implementation. Operate the experimental system in real or simulated form for testing and debugging purposes. Modify elements which fail to perform according to specifications, and operate the proposed system in parallel with the existing system to test it under operating conditions.
6. Evaluation. Review the results of simulation or parallel operation to refine the final design, correct deficiencies and develop the operating version.

The systems study is normally conceived as a special project. When the task is completed the study ends. This is often the best approach to systems analysis, but consideration should be given to the design of monitoring systems within the target system. This monitoring subsystem becomes a part of the management subsystem and is used to provide data reflecting the state of the system so that corrective measures can be applied when deviations from established standards occur. The objective is to work toward the concept of a self-organizing system which delivers feedback information from regular operations into the monitoring system so that an "early warning" signal indicates the need to work on a problem before a crisis develops.

Selected Readings

Burns, Robert W., Jr. 1971. A generalized methodology for library systems analysis. *College and research libraries* 32: 295-303.

Chapman, Edward A., St. Pierre, Paul L., and Lubans, John, Jr. 1970. Systems in a library. In *Library systems analysis guidelines,* pp. 7-17. New York: Wiley.

Fasana, Paul J. 1973. Systems analysis. *Library trends* 21: 465-78.

Leimkuhler, F. F. 1973. Large scale library systems. *Library trends* 21:575-86.

Management Information Service. 1968. *Introduction to systems analysis.* Washington, D.C.: International City Manager's Association.

Pratt, Allan D. 1969. Systems, components, characteristics and analysis. In *Library use of computers: an introduction,* ed. Gloria L. Smith and Robert S. Meyer, pp. 19-26. SLA Monograph no. 3. New York: SLA.

Salton, Gerard. 1975. Library system analysis. In *Dynamic information and library processing,* pp. 163-214. Englewood Cliffs, N.J.: Prentice-Hall.

3. Stating goals and objectives

Goals and objectives are the most important elements of systems analysis. These serve both the managers and the members of an organization. They provide a view to the future by showing where the organization is going and a look backward to show what has been accomplished. The importance of these two functions cannot be overemphasized.

Why are goals and objectives significant?
The statement of goals and objectives is significant because they provide the basis for evaluating the performance of the total system. Churchman (86:29) indicates that the management scientist considers it very important to keep in mind "... the total systems objectives, and, more specifically, the performance measures of the whole system. ..." Fasana (121:469) reiterates this notion of performance measurement:

Unless objectives are stated explicitly, it is impossible to develop measures of performance. Unless effective measures of performance can be demonstrated, it is difficult to justify continued levels of financial support and impossible to argue for increased support to provide for new or additional services. . . .

In *Introduction to Systems Analysis,* prepared by John K. Parker for the International City Managers Association (223:6), the same argument is repeated in a slightly different form:

> Once the need (for the service or product) has been determined, the process of systems analysis focuses on translating the statement of need into a detailed definition of objectives.
>
> . . . In this step, the need is converted into a number of measurable situations which, when achieved, will satisfy the need. This involves thinking through the details of what is actually desired and how to judge whether the desired condition has been achieved.

It becomes clear that those who have experienced the need to measure the performance of an organization find the statement of goals critical in the evaluation of performance. The only further consideration we may need is a clarification of the terminology.

Since the dictionary definition of these terms identifies each of them in terms of the other—a goal is an objective and an objective is a goal—it is not much help, and we may need to look at the way the terms are used. For example, in setting behavioral objectives in education, the purpose of the objective is to find a measure which is not subject to different interpretations by different teachers, but is consistently measurable by all teachers. The sum of these objectives within a course contributes to the achievement of the goal defined for the course. Similarly, each course as it achieves its objectives contributes to the goal of an educational program.

The definition of objectives as intermediate steps toward a larger goal relates the meanings of the two terms. Ackoff turns this definition around so that the goal is the immediate end of the organization and the objective becomes the remote and to some degree unattainable end (1). Thus, it is essential to express goals and objectives carefully so that the use of the terms is clear.

It is also important to establish goals and objectives that are feasible for the specific organization and to provide a precise way of measuring the achievement of these established goals and objectives. It is less important to be concerned about which term is used than it is to be concerned about the statement of purpose for the organization and the definition of measures which will demonstrate success or failure in the effort to fulfill that purpose.

It would be unrealistic, for example, for a public library to establish as one of its goals the registration of one hundred percent of the members of the community it serves. While this may be an "ideal," to use Ackoff's term, it is only possible to approximate it. The preferred approach is to set the immediate objective at five or ten percent above the previous registration level for the first year. When this figure is achieved, it can be revised upward to provide the next objective. This is the sense which Ackoff conveys when he views the objective as an ideal to be sought.

Regardless of the terminology used—and use needs to be consistent within an organization—the difficult task comes in preparing the statement of goals and objectives.

What are the problems in analyzing
the goals and objectives of an organization?

Katz and Kahn have indicated some of the problems of analyzing organizations in general, and, in particular, of identifying the purposes of organizations:

> . . . common sense approaches to understanding and altering organizations are ancient and perpetual. They tend, on the whole, to rely heavily on two assumptions: that the location and nature of an organization are given by its name; and that an organization is possessed of built-in goals—because such goals were implanted by its founders, decreed by its present leaders, or because they

emerged mysteriously as the purposes of the organizational system itself. These assumptions scarcely provide an adequate basis for the study of organizations and can at times be misleading even fallacious . . . (177:14)

Interviews are commonly used to gather data relating to the goals and objectives of an organization. In discussing three levels of interviews for this purpose, Robinson indicates the nature of the problem:

[The systems analyst] may be surprised to find that policy-makers and management do not share a common view of the organization's objectives. Perhaps the request for a statment of objectives will cause some embarrassment, for it is possible that the objectives of a library may be difficult to define. However, a statment of objectives must be agreed, in quantitative terms if possible. The analyst should not be surprised to find that management and "workers" disagree over the functional tasks carried out, nor that a worker's description of his job does not tally with the observed facts. (281:3)

One of the major difficulties that occurs in analyzing goals and objectives is tradition. Many organizations, libraries among them, were begun in response to philosophical assumptions involving moral imperatives, e.g., the state should provide education for its future citizens, a library should provide for the educational and cultural edification of its citizens. More important is what the organization is to achieve as the outcome of what it does with its resources. We are not very adept at measuring educational and cultural edification, for these are subjective elements which only the individual can assess (and may do so inaccurately). The need is for empirical measures of service which indicate the achievement of goals consistently and indicate the performance of the total system.

Buckland in his *Book Availability and the Library User* (59) demonstrates the need to revise our view of goals and objectives as well as the need for empirical measures to indicate the achievement of goals. The librarian has always considered the availability of books a primary goal of the library; however, it has been necessary, first, to develop some means of bibliographic control to identify the existence of individual works, and, second, to develop some means of determining their relevance to a particular user's needs. These developments were necessary to build library collections and to organize them in usable ways. Following the shift from information scarcity to information surplus which took place in the twentieth century, the critical element shifts as well from identifying a work for a user's needs to delivering the book to the user. Buckland in his study of book availability analyzes the operation of the library of the University of Lancaster and shows that there are variables—loan policy and duplication policy—which can be used to improve the availability of books in the university library.

Using a combination of variable loan and duplication policies, it becomes possible to keep the provision of library materials responsive to change, but it requires continuous monitoring of collection information to provide the feedback needed to apply adaptive controls. In the past, librarians needed to direct their attention to the objectives of bibliographic control to achieve the goal of book availability; in the present, librarians need to complement the efforts to maintain bibliographic control by directing their attention to user needs and the dynamics of supply and demand.

Selected Readings

Carlson, Robert D., and Lewis, James A. 1973. Definition of systems and project specifications. In *The systems analysis workbook: a complete guide to project implementation and control,* pp. 39–45. Englewood Cliffs, N.J.: Prentice-Hall.

Hamburg, Morris, et al. 1972. Library objectives and performance measures and their use in decision making. *Library quarterly* 42:107–28.

Kelly, William F. 1969. The field of systems and procedures. In *Management through systems and procedures: the total systems concept,* pp. 3-13. New York: Wiley.

Robinson, F., et al. 1969. *Symplegades: systems analysis in libraries.* Newcastle upon Tyne, England: Oriel Press.

Van Gigch, John P. 1974. Goals, priorities, and tradeoffs. In *Applied general systems theory,* pp. 79-106. New York: Harper and Row.

4. Methods of description

Methods of description and systems engineering are the key components of the systems study. The techniques treated in this work cover the diagnostic processes used to identify dysfunctional elements in the system and the prescriptive processes used to design or redesign the system. The techniques are best viewed as reiterative processes. Each element—organization, forms and files, equipment, and budget—is analyzed separately. The results of the analysis are then evaluated in relation to the total system. As each element is completed and related to the overall system, further modifications may be required, until the complete system is designed.

Organization is the structure which supports all other activities. The objective in designing an organization is to provide the best distribution of work according to similarity of activities, geographic location, types of client, or, in libraries, subjects. The organization provides the means of coordinating work, issuing orders, and evaluating progress. Kelly (181:32) suggests eight criteria that are useful in analyzing organizations: effectiveness, division of work, delegation of authority and responsibility, control factors, channels of contact, proportionate composition, flexibility, and perpetual existence.

Since there are no fixed benchmarks for determining an exact organizational pattern, the evaluation rests on comparisons with other similar types of organization and judgment of the situation under study. Sensitivity to the human factors in work situations will contribute greatly to this analysis.

Forms and Files. Every organization operates on large quantities of information and data. The way in which the information is gathered and stored has many different effects on the work being done. A form is a document with fixed information preprinted and space for variable information to be added at the time and place a transaction takes place. The order of the information on the form and the clarity of design facilitate the recording process and thus reduce the time required for each transaction. Since forms are a means of recording data, the information is often taken from the form as input for a subsequent procedure. Arranging the data to facilitate transcription in subsequent procedures contributes again to reduced processing time and further cost savings.

The advantage of forms as time savers sometimes works against itself. Forms often proliferate without control or evaluation of their role in the system. Duplication occurs, which adds to paper and printing costs, to storage costs, and to supply control costs. The effective control of forms requires a central point at which all new forms are reviewed in relation to function, to other existing forms, and to applications in particular procedures.

An important aspect of forms control is the disposition of each form. More often than not a form ends in a file. Sometimes the file develops because the form is there. Each file represents additional costs for filing, storage equipment, and space. The files must be evaluated according to the frequency of their use, alternative sources for the information, and the cost of locating the information when it is needed. These costs can accumulate to large sums of money when the organization is large. Consequently, forms need regular review to determine the need for each file and its contribution to system effectiveness.

Some records may entail legal obligations and the retention of the record and the file may be determined by law. The effective control of records requires a catalog of all files being maintained in the system which indicates retention periods and provides for systematic withdrawal and destruction of obsolete documents. The records management function is best coordinated with archival considerations so that documents of historical value can be identified and retained regardless of legal or system requirements.

Equipment. When library technology was limited to a few typewriters, a very small part of the resources were used for equipment purchase or acquisition. As the technology becomes more sophisticated, costs increase proportionately. Computers, of course, represent significant expenditures and will undoubtedly become more important for all libraries in the near future. There are two types of cost associated with equipment: systems costs and purchase costs.

Systems costs are analyzed during the design of specific procedures and equipment applications. Over and above these costs are purchase costs, which are usually included in start-up costs of a new system and amortized over five or ten years. The acquisition of major equipment requires the expenditure of large amounts of money. In many budgeting situations, such expenditures are difficult to obtain in a single budget year. Two alternatives are available: leasing to purchase and straight leasing. Medium range equipment in the five to ten thousand dollar range may be purchased advantageously by a lease to purchase agreement in which the lease payments are credited to the purchase of the equipment. There is a cost over the purchase price for financing the purchase agreement in most cases, and the decision may be based on budgeting considerations rather than actual cost advantages. It may be possible, for example, to obtain equipment through lease-to-purchase plans when outright purchase would be impossible.

Straight leasing, of course, simply entails a cost for the use of the equipment for as long as the equipment serves its purpose. When the system changes or new equipment is developed, the equipment can be returned and replaced with more appropriate items. This is very useful in computer applications where equipment changes rapidly. The important task is to assess cost accurately so that the actual operating costs of the system are clearly known. This is essential for comparing the costs of alternative methods and for developing budget requests. Since most budgeting occurs in annual intervals, the determination of costs in advance of the budget request becomes imperative for systems implementation.

Budget. All of the preceeding elements relate to the budget. The organization determines the number and level of personnel that are needed to perform the work of the organization, and are translated into salary and benefit costs. The salary is an obvious cost item. Benefit costs—health insurance, social security payments, retirement fund payments, etc.—are significant budget items running a minimum of nine to twelve percent of the nominal salary figure. In most libraries, the personnel costs account for seventy to seventy-five percent of the operating costs. The thirty to twenty-five percent remaining must cover all other costs.

When the library budget for materials—books, periodicals, binding, films, recordings, etc.—is subtracted from this twenty-five or thirty percent of the total budget, it becomes very clear that the justification of equipment, file storage equipment, and other nonpersonnel items is a very important part of budget preparation. Generally, the justification of equipment will be contingent on its effectiveness in delaying or eliminating the need for additional staff. While some intangible elements of the application—increased speed, greater accuracy—receive consideration, the effective justification is cost reduction.

Organization, forms and files, and equipment are interrelated elements of a system and are closely related to the budget. Each must be examined carefully to determine how it contributes to system effectiveness. When the elements have been reviewed and effective combinations selected, the parts of the system must be integrated into the most effective total system. Integration is accomplished only after the systems engineering elements are incorporated into the design.

Some of the elements included in the systems study have been indicated. A number of items recur in the application of systems analysis to libraries; two are considered below.

Why is it important to use several different types of studies to analyze all of the aspects of an operation?

In *Operations Mangement,* the authors summarize the need for an overall view of the system:

> An aggregate, or overall view of the system enables us to understand the role of systems components. A total system is defined by its boundaries. An operating system may be viewed as a black box which produces a set of outputs from its inputs. Primary inputs are materials, energy or information. Secondary inputs are auxiliaries such as supplies or services. Primary outputs are goods and services produced. Secondary outputs are the by-products of the operations. (174:85)

This concept of the overall view is elaborated on with the indication that more detailed analysis is required for each of the system components: "... the aggregate, or overall view of the system holds the center of the stage (in the beginning). ... Later we shall take a closer, more detailed look at the internal characteristics and rules of operation governing the components ... " (174:64).

As this notion is continued, specific types of analysis are treated, e.g., facilities location and layout analysis, comparable to selecting a library site and designing the layout for efficient operations. Next, it is the design of systems which keeps operations functioning: "The relationship of sub-systems to the larger system is not always easy to determine, but organizing its contributions to optimize the total system is crucial" (174:171).

> The systems concept focuses on the relationships of these parts or subsystems and how their performance affects the whole system. Under a systems approach, one

changes his view of organization from looking at structures to looking at flows and processes. Systems theory is
concerned with dynamics, flows, and interrelationships
rather than static hierarchies with traditional linkages.
. . . (216:20)

Since the various subsystems are contributing to the overall system objectives, it becomes necessary to analyze all of
the component subsystems in relation to the overall system.
Each of these component subsystems, however, has different
characteristics and requires different types of analytical
treatment. It is this variety of methods which raises the
question of the analyst performing the system study.

*What are the advantages and disadvantages
of training the librarian to perform the analytical studies?*

Since each librarian brings a unique combination of knowledge, skills, and abilities to his profession, this question can
only be considered in relative terms. In order to determine the
advantages and disadvantages of training the librarian in
systems work, it is necessary to consider the qualifications a
systems analyst must demonstrate to accomplish his task.
There are at least four primary characteristics needed by
the effective systems analyst: creativity, conceptual and analytical ability, and the ability to work with details. Supple-
menting these, we would look for logic, accuracy, and
persistence. While improvements can be accomplished by
careful analysis of operating systems, the significant contribution is creativity. This quality brings with it the ability to
discover novel solutions to problems and to create genuinely
new systems. Creativity must be combined with conceptual
skill, which aids the analyst in visualizing the structure and
the relationships between components in the overall design;
it also aids the analyst in anticipating the effects of possible
alternatives to the existing system. The detailed analysis
comes next. The discovery of alternatives is not the same as a
solution; they must be analyzed in detail and tested against
the real system. Logical ability is related to analytical skill

and may be synonymous in many ways. Accuracy is essential, for it is no solution if errors are allowed to distort the expected results. Without persistence, the analyst may be easily convinced that the solution is unworkable. He must listen with caution to the concert of noes that often greet the novel (and best) solution and proceed to analyze the alternatives in detail. Having discovered a flaw in the first approximation, he may need to persist through several reiterations to verify the potential or lack of potential for a given alternative. Other characteristics might be included in the list, but these are sufficient to consider the advantages and disadvantages of training the librarian to perform the studies.

The two primary advantages of training librarians for systems work in libraries are knowledge of the library and its functions and availability. From his education and experience, the librarian understands the operations of the library, will be familiar with the literature and the solutions that have worked in other libraries, and will be familiar with the goals of the library. Assuming that he is a member of the existing staff, he will be available for the several stages of the systems study from initiation to implementation and evaluation. He will also be available for periodic reviews of the systems to assess their continuing effectiveness in providing the performance originally intended.

The advantages may also be the disadvantages: the librarian is indoctrinated with "the library way of doing things" and may be too easily lulled into rationalizing the currently accepted methods used in his own and other libraries. Unless his systems responsibility becomes his primary concern, it may be difficult to take time from regular duties to do systems work. Such sporadic efforts lose momentum and frequently fail because they are not given the emphasis that is needed. Finally, the systems study, whether the responsibility of a librarian on the staff, a systems person on the staff, or an outside analyst, entails costs for the library. The final decision must rest on an evaluation of the cost/benefit analysis of the alternatives. The completion of a systems study is itself a system and must be viewed in relation to other components of the library as a system.

Selected Readings

American Library Association. 1965-. *Library technology reports.*

ASLIB Research Department. 1970. The analysis of library processes. *Journal of documentation* 26:30-45.

Chapman, Edward A., et al. 1970. Analysis phase of the systems study—current procedures. In *Library systems analysis guidelines,* pp. 45-64. New York: Wiley.

Deming, Donald D., and Murdock, R. G. 1967. Equipment replacement analysis. In *Handbook of business administration, ed. H. B. Maynard, pp. 7.65-7.74. New York: McGraw-Hill.*

Dougherty, Richard M., and Heinritz, Fred J. 1966. Forms: their analysis, control and design. In *Scientific management of library operations,* pp. 79-98. New York: Scarecrow.

Hayes, Robert M., and Becker Joseph 1974. Methods of system description. In *Handbook of data processing for libraries,* pp. 145-77. Los Angeles: Melville.

Kelly, William F. 1969. Standards for the evaluation of organizational structures; Forms—kinds and design; Forms creation. In *Management through systems and procedures: the total systems concept,* pp. 31-45; 209-60; and 261-75. New York: Wiley.

Millard, Patricia, comp. 1966. *Modern library equipment.* London: Crosby Lockwood & Son.

Myres, Gibbs. 1968. Forms design and control. In *Systems and procedures: a handbook for business and industry,* ed. Victor Lazzaro. 2d ed. Englewood Cliffs, N.J.: Prentice-Hall.

Pfiffner, John M. and Lane, Owen S. 1964. Organizational survey; Equipment survey; and Budget analysis. In *A manual for administrative analysis, pp. 19-26; 42-46; 47-50; 72-79. Los Angeles: University of Southern California Press.*

5. Systems engineering

Systems engineering in one sense is the culmination of developments initiated by Taylor and the scientific management movement. In another sense, it is the beginning of a new phase of industrial engineering brought about by the changes in production facilities from combinations of single function units (e.g., drilling, machining, milling, etc.) to present-day forms of automated production systems. The underlying elements in both of these views of systems engineering are the detailed analysis of task components, precise measurement of labor and equipment costs, and the use of simulation techniques to determine probable outcomes under varying conditions. A comprehensive treatment of systems engineering is beyond the scope of this tract; instead it will be sufficient to distinguish between those techniques applied to very large operations and those suitable for small organizations. Emphasis is placed on those techniques which have the most value for the small and medium size library: work sampling, work simplification, and charting techniques.

Systems engineering evolved from industrial engineering. Until the Second World War, much of the industrial engineering effort was directed toward refinements of work measurement, methods engineering (finding the one best way) and the development of assembly line production systems. At the same time, the costs of production were shifting from direct to indirect costs as the composition of the labor force changed from predominantly production workers to predominantly office employees. These changes led to the use of industrial engineering methods for the analysis of office operations.

During and following World War II, experience with project management and operations research led to the development of several techniques for analyzing operations. These methods—which include the Delphi Technique, linear and dynamic programming, PERT, queuing, simulation, and others—have become part of the techniques used in systems engineering, management science, and systems analysis. Their development depended in some measure on the availability of digital computers that could handle the extensive computation needed in the analysis of large operations. The digital computer also contributed to these developments because of the need for analytical techniques for designing information-handling systems. A brief summary of the techniques will provide a perspective from which we can examine a few in greater detail.

The *Delphi Technique* is a predictive method which elicits responses from experts on their expectations for future developments in a particular field. The responses are tabulated and edited into a coherent picture of the future. This is followed by a new questionnaire and the results of the first questionnaire so that the individuals may refine their first estimates. None of the individuals knows who the other experts are, and each presents his own perception of the future. After several rounds a fairly clear indication of future directions emerges. It is a probable future reflecting the thinking of knowledgeable persons in the field and has proved valuable under many conditions.

PERT (*Program Evaluation and Review Technique*) originated as a scheduling technique and has been used successfully for ongoing operations as well. It uses network-charting methods with the nodes indicating events in a project or operation and the links indicating activities. Individuals responsible for each activity estimate the best, worst, and most likely times for each activity, which are then combined into an expected time. In most networks of this type, there is a critical path through the network which can be used to monitor progress on a project. Refinements in the method are referred to as PERT/CPM or simply CPM. The importance of PERT lies in its ability to detect the need for reallocating resources to activities falling behind schedule. It has been credited with saving eighteen to twenty-four months on the development of the Polaris missile system.

Linear and dynamic programming perform similar functions for different classes of operating situations. In linear programming, the situations are essentially additive; dynamic programming is used for operations demonstrating more complex relationships. An example of additive forms of operation is given by Hostrop (160:113) for a library where twice as many books require twice as much shelf space. When linear situations are plotted on a graph, the result is a straight line. In operations where straight line relationships do not hold, it is necessary to use dynamic programming.

Simulation uses the results of linear and dynamic programming to experiment with different operating conditions. The mathematical expressions derived from the analysis for linear and dynamic programming describe the operating situation as realistically as possible. With the computer, these equations can be run and rerun with different combinations of input to see what kind of result can be expected. Since the simulation runs use minutes to represent months or years of real time, the simulation may run far into the future with a simulated outcome for the operation. The difficult task is to develop a set of mathematical statements which closely approximates the real situation.

For example, in the analysis of operations of the University of Lancaster Library, it was necessary to examine the relationship between the convenience and inconvenience of short and long loan periods for a user who has a book and a user who wants a book. A long loan policy is convenient for the user who has a book and inconvenient for a user who wants the same book, but a short loan policy is inconvenient for a user who has a book and convenient for the user who wants the same book. Buckland summarizes the simulation used to analyze the relationship (59:68–73) and provides the documentation and programs for the simulation studies carried out at Lancaster (66).

While all of these techniques can be used for large or small operations, it is often not feasible to use them when the benefits will be small. Consequently, in many libraries the simpler methods of work measurement—work sampling, work simplification, and charting techniques—can be more immediately productive for improving costs and operational effectiveness. To this end, then, let us consider these methods of analyzing library systems.

Work sampling tells us how much it costs in work hours to complete a transaction. *Work simplification* gives us a means of finding better ways to complete the transaction. *Charting* provides a method of communicating the results of our work simplification studies. When these three techniques are combined in the systems study, we have completed the diagnostic part of the process and we have a stock of possible changes that may be used in the design or prescriptive phase of the study.

Work measurement is the sensitive area of systems analysis. This technique shows the actual costs and is a measure of productivity in the organization. It becomes sensitive because the traditional approach to work measurement has been used to establish piecework rates in industry. Since the manager's goal was to produce at the lowest cost, piecework rates were often lowered when time studies showed faster production was possible. Few clerical operations lend themselves to piecework pricing. Consequently, *work sampling* is the most frequently used method of work measurement. It has the advantage of requiring little training, of being distributive—that is, of measuring the work of the group rather than the individual—and of being simple in execution.

Work measurement results are used for two purposes: to compare the costs of alternative methods and to compute work hours required for each activity. The work computations are then translated into personal services costs for the budget request. Work measurement costs must be supplemented with equipment costs and material costs, e.g., forms, chemicals, etc., when comparing costs of alternative methods. These costs are directly related to the budget process. Since the major expenditure is for personal services, the underlying goal in every organization is to find methods of accomplishing the work which require less time. The growing need for better cost data in libraries generates increasing interest in work measurement. The question we turn to next is a common one when libraries become involved in systems studies.

What characteristics of work sampling have contributed to the method's popularity in library systems studies?

The most important characteristics of work sampling for libraries are simplicity and efficiency. Time study as it developed with Taylor and Gilbreth was used in production situations involving large volume. Small savings in time for each item accumulated to large savings for a plant over a period of time. The traditional methods of time study required a considerable investment in man power and this investment was considered worthwhile because of the cost savings that could be achieved. In library situations, the volume of processing is occasionally large enough to warrant an investment in time study, but the probable savings seldom justify the expense required for precision studies using stopwatch methods. Furthermore, these studies require experience and training in stopwatch methods before accuracy can reach acceptable levels.

In contrast to the requirements for stopwatch studies, work sampling can be accomplished with much smaller investments in staff time and with much less training. At the same time, using statistical techniques, the level of accuracy can be kept high enough to meet the library's requirements. These levels of accuracy can be adjusted according to the study— increasing the sample size for greater accuracy or relaxing the level of confidence for less critical situations. The combination of lower costs and less intensive training to carry out work sampling studies has contributed to their popularity in library systems studies. One use of work measurement is to identify the activities which use the greatest number of work hours. These activities become the first candidates for work simplification studies because the probability of saving time and resources is greater in these activities.

Work simplification is the systematic study of every task or activity performed in an organization in order to determine the best way of completing the task. It is often referred to as "procedures analysis" and may occasionally be what is meant when the phrase "systems analysis" is used. It is based on very simple concepts. Each task is analyzed by examining what is being done in the present system. The task is then reviewed by asking a series of questions: e.g., Is this task necessary? Can it be done better at a different time or place, or by a different person? Is this method the best one for the task?

Most systems analysts use the classic who, what, where, when, how, and why to identify the elements of the task. When all these questions are answered, the task is completely identified within the context of the system. While it is useful to ask first why it is done, the six questions are related and need to be considered compositely in the design of a new method. Since work simplification is used in limited and in extended systems studies, we consider some of the reasons for its use in our next question.

What are the common characteristics of work simplification's use for limited and comprehensive systems studies?

The underlying goal of work simplification is to eliminate all unnecessary effort. Since this is the goal of systems analysis, within the constraints of overall systems objectives, the characteristics of work simplification are common to all studies regardless of their scope. They can be represented as a series of three questions: (1) Is this procedure necessary? (2) Is this step in this procedure necessary? and (3) Is this step accomplished with the least effort? These questions are reiterated as many times as necessary to encompass the limits of the study. The process can be shown by a sequence of questions and decisions:

1. Define the limits of the study.
2. Identify the tasks in the study and list them.
3. Beginning with the first task:
   a. Is this task necessary?
   b. If the answer is no, proceed to the next question.
   c. If the answer is yes, list the task and proceed to the next question.
   d. Is this the last task?
   e. If the answer is no, take the next task and go back to number three.
4. Beginning with the first step in the first task:
   a. Is this step necessary?
   b. If the answer is no, proceed.
   c. If the answer is yes, list the step and proceed.
   d. Is this the last step in this task?
   e. If the answer is no, return to number four and repeat for the next step in this task.
   f. If the answer is yes, return to number four and repeat for the next task.
   g. If the answer is yes, proceed.
5. Beginning with the first (necessary) step in the first (necessary) task:
   a. Is this step completed with the least effort?
   b. If the answer is no:
      (1) analyze the step
      (2) find alternative methods
      (3) repeat until answer is yes
      (4) proceed.
   c. Is this the last step in this task?
   d. If the answer is yes, proceed.
   e. If the answer is no, return to number five and repeat for the next step.
   f. Is this the last task?
   g. If the answer is yes, proceed.
   h. If the answer is no, return to number five and repeat for the next task.
6. Design new system.

While this captures the essence of the work simplification process, it is clearly a very abbreviated form of the analysis. Disregarding, for the moment, that someone considers every step in every task a necessary one, it becomes evident that each of these steps must be subjected to a critical examination. This analysis is accomplished by applying the principles of motion economy to each step (108:66). These principles developed by Taylor, Gilbreth, Barnes, and others must be extended in several ways. The task of eliminating unnecessary motion remains, but the questions may have to be revised to cover the collection and recording of unnecessary information, the preparation of reports that are no longer needed, or the maintenance of unnecessary files. This moves the analysis back one step from the actual motions used to the need for the step in the process. The objective is the same, however, and to some degree the notion of least effort can be translated into least time. While changes made by eliminating steps clearly reduce the time needed for a particular task, changes in methods may result in savings that are less apparent. In order to compare the alternative methods, we need some way to measure them. We have seen that work measurement can be used to compare alternative methods. Another way of comparing methods is by charting the flow of transactions and records used in a procedure, and we consider these techniques next.

The verbal description of a clerical procedure can become extremely complex. When an analyst begins asking the questions about a task or procedure, he begins to accumulate large quantities of data related to the task. This is often true for tasks which appear to be very simple. *Charting techniques* evolved as a shorthand method of communicating the significant details of a procedure. The graphic techniques have been standardized so that an analyst reviewing studies that have been documented in standard form can learn the process quickly and accurately.

The charts can also be used in training situations to show the details of a procedure to new employees. The advantage of the chart is the ability to get an overall view of the process and still have the details available when specific questions occur. This combination of detail and summary is less readily available in written form. It is often necessary to have verbal descriptions, however, to supplement the charts.

Charts are referred to by a number of names. A system flow chart shows in less detail all of the processes and procedures that are part of a system. Procedures charts may take a single transaction and enlarge the detail so that all aspects of the task are identified. These charts may be supplemented by layout charts showing the work space in plan with the files and equipment indicated within the work area. Both are often supplemented by work distribution charts or linear responsibility charts which indicate the office or individual responsible for each task. Our next question considers the varieties of charts and their use in system studies.

*What kinds of charts are available
to the systems analyst?*

Dougherty and Gull have described the charting techniques used in systems analysis (108, 143). The following list modifies some of the descriptions in the literature to conform to recent developments. The types of chart are arranged in three basic categories according to their use for depicting: (1) process or operations, (2) personnel and task relationships, and (3) scheduling and control elements.

1. Charts showing process or operations
   a. Flowchart or operational flow chart: shows steps taken to complete a task or procedure.
   b. Process chart: shows the operations used in a task or procedure using printed forms and standard ASME symbols.
   c. Schematic flowchart: uses abbreviated indications of a process to indicate the highlights. Often uses pictorial symbols and may be used in presentations of proposed systems.
   d. Forms flowchart: shows the flow of information from one form to another by means of copies of completed forms.

e. Forms distribution charts: emphasizes the flow of forms through organizational units and provides limited operational description.

f. Logical or block diagrams: shows the logic and steps used to complete a data processing job with computers.

g. Layout flowchart: combines space arrangements with the flow of forms in the physical space.

h. Right hand–left hand charts and SIMO charts: The right and left hand chart shows the motion of both hands at each step in a process and are used in method studies. The SIMO (Simultaneous Motion) chart shows the same kinds of relationships and are characteristic of micromotion studies.

i. The HIPO package: The HIPO package—Hierarchical Input Processing Output—consists of a hierarchically defined function chart and an input-processing-output chart (178). The combination of hierarchical and process charts begins at the system level and is repeated for each level of the hierarchy. The technique is designed for use with structured or top-down programming techniques used in the design of large systems.

j. Data flow diagrams: developed by Yourdon, Inc. and used as an integral part of Yourdon's structured methodology which proceeds from structured analysis to structured design. The data flow diagram, also known as a bubble chart, shows the way data is moved through the system. At the analysis stage, the programming technique to perform specific operations is ignored until the data flow and data requirements for the entire system have been identified (336).

2. Charts showing personnel and task relationships

a. Organizational chart: the most common type of chart showing the channels of communication and the lines of responsibility.

b. Linear responsibility chart: shows the specific responsibility of managers and supervisors in particular procedures. (N. B. this chart was copyrighted by Serge A. Birns in 1953.)

   c. Work distribution or work analysis chart: shows staff (horizontal axis) and activities (vertical axis) for an organizational unit with the responsibility and average time for each person involved in an activity.

3. Charts showing schedules

   a. Gantt charts: plots time on the horizontal axis for projects or parts of projects arranged on the vertical axis so that progress toward completion can be indicated at regular intervals.

   b. PERT chart (Program Evaluation Review Techniques): uses a network chart to show events (nodes) and time (links) each event is expected to take.

   While standards for chart symbols have been adopted by the American National Standards Institute, some variations still occur.

What are the essential symbols used in flowcharts to chart the steps the analyst uses in work simplification?

The IBM pamphlet, *Flowcharting Techniques* (165:9), indicates the basic symbols for processing, input/output, flow or connection, and annotation as the least number of required symbols. Two symbols must be added to these to provide a flexible system of charting: the decision box and the connector symbol. With these six symbols, it is possible to chart all of the operations in a system regardless of the level of complexity.

The methods of analysis and the techniques of systems engineering are combined in the systems study. A typical study is carried out in two major phases: the analysis and the design phases. During the first phase, each element of the system is analyzed, described, and documented. These results are used to identify the areas where change appears to be possible and productive. Typically, the analyst focuses on tasks involving high volume and high costs.

The analyst begins designing the new system·by considering all of the possible alternatives. This is the creative phase. Combinations of method and equipment are explored, tested, or simulated. Gradually, decisions are made at broad levels and the new system is put together in a preliminary form. A process of change, evaluation, and revision takes place at this point and continues until the final design is evolved.

The design phase leads to the implementation of the system. It is wise to run the new and the old systems simultaneously until all the problems are resolved and the new system is operating. Occasionally, it is impossible to continue parallel operations and implementation is accomplished in stages. Each stage is installed and debugged before implementing the next stage. When the system is operating, the final step is an evaluation. The system becomes the operating system and is incorporated into the regular schedule of system review.

Selected Readings

Bellomy, Fred L. 1969. Management planning for library system development. *Journal of library automation* 2:187-217.

Bohl, Marilyn. 1971. *Flow-Charting techniques.* Chicago: Science Research Associates.

Bolles, S. W. 1967. The use of flow-charts in the analysis of library operations. *Special libraries* 58:95-98.

Brush, William H. 1968. Work measurement. In *Systems and procedures: a handbook for business and industry,* ed. Victor Lazarro, pp. 143-81. Englewood Cliffs, N. J.: Prentice-Hall.

Cavender, T. P. 1965. Time and motion techniques related to costs of expanding the card catalog. *Library resources and technical services* 1:104-108.

Chapman, Edward A., St. Pierre, Paul, and Lubans, John, Jr. 1970. Flow charting. In *Library systems analysis guidelines,* pp. 86-88. New York: Wiley.

Dougherty, Richard M. 1970. Is work simplification alive and well someplace? *American libraries* 2:969-71.

Dougherty, Richard M., and Heinritz, Fred J. 1966. Decision flow charting; The flow process chart, flow diagram and block diagram; Time study; Sampling. In *Scientific management of library operations,* pp. 52–65; 35–51; 99–114; and 115–35. New York: Scarecrow.

Everts, Harry F. 1967. *Introduction to PERT.* Boston, Mass.: Allyn and Bacon Inc.

Farino, Mario V. 1970. *Flowcharting.* Englewood Cliffs, N.J.: Prentice-Hall.

Gimbel, Henning. 1969. *Work simplification in Danish public libraries.* Trans. Randolph C. Ellsworth. Chicago: ALA.

Goodell;, John S. 1975. *Libraries and work sampling.* Littleton, Colo.: Libraries Unlimited.

Gull, C. D. 1968. Logical flow charts and other new techniques for the administration of libraries and information centers. *Library resources and technical services* 12:47–66.

Newmaier, Richard, and Mullee, William. 1968. Work simplification. In *Systems and procedures: a handbook for business and industry,* ed. Victor Lazzaro, pp. 123–42. Englewood Cliffs, N. J.: Prentice-Hall.

Pomeroy, Richard W. 1968. Systems charting. In *Systems and procedures: a handbook for business and industry,* Ed. Victor Lazzaro. Englewood Cliffs, N. J.: Prentice-Hall.

Wallace, W. Lyle, 1962. *Work simplification.* Systems Education Monograph no. 1. Detroit, Mich.: Systems and Procedures Association.

Woodruff, Elaine. 1957. Work measurement applied to libraries. *Special libraries* 48:139–44.

6. Evolution of computers

Digital computers offer the most challenging and exciting prospect for libraries and information systems. They do not solve all the problems inherent in the management of large stores of knowledge, but they do relieve humans of many of the routine tasks that are a part of knowledge management systems. We would be very upset if a construction foreman made his workers carry steel beams to the top of a twenty-story building on a series of inclined ramps, yet we are not particularly concerned that thousands of workers are required to record and to manipulate millions of pieces of information by hand. The use of human capabilities to perform trivial tasks is one of the least desirable outcomes of the Industrial Revolution. The prospect of the electronic revolution is the opportunity to transform work into more meaningful tasks, and the digital computer is one of the tools which will make this possible.

In our examination of the computer, we shall consider first the elements of computer systems, then explore the ways in which computers have evolved since their development in the 1940s, and, finally, how present trends may contribute to further applications in libraries and information systems. In this examination, however, we consider only the digital computer. Analog computers, which are used to convert physical phenomena into approximate numerical form, appear to have little importance in library applications at the present time. We begin, then, by reviewing the elements of computer systems.

Although the commercial computer is only about twenty-five years old, the present models bear as little resemblence to the original computers as present-day space vehicles bear to early airplanes. Computer systems consist of three elements: hardware, software, and applications. The hardware is the equipment which performs the actual operations, software is the programs—sets of instructions—which direct the computer to perform specific operations in a particular sequence. Applications are the jobs the computer is used to accomplish. In this chapter we consider only the hardware. The software is treated next in the chapter on programming languages. Applications are treated in the chapter on library automation.

As computers have evolved from the cumbersome devices of the early 1950s to their present form, they have become much more common in our society. As a result, there is a continuing pressure on the librarian to use them in the library. To the layman, it seems obvious that the computer can keep track of the library's records more rapidly and more accurately than has been possible in the past. The solution to the library's problems have been less obvious to the librarian.

How has the development of the computer contributed to its application in the library?

The early digital computers were designed to perform mathematical calculations for scientific and technical problems. These computers had no facilities for handling alphabetic characters or handled them with difficulty. Since the 1950s, when commercial computers first became available, alphanumeric processing has gradually been extended, but the limitations of input-output devices, limited storage capacities, and mathematically oriented programming languages mitigated against applications in libraries. The decade of the 1960s showed definite changes in this situation. The input-output devices were refined, operating systems improved, and business oriented programming languages emerged. The computing facility changed slowly and gradually from a computation laboratory to an information processing facility. Hayes summarizes these developments as follows:

> ... the last 20 years have witnessed a rapidly increasing interest among librarians concerning the possibility of using punched card machines and, more recently, computers to carry out many library functions. The reasons are clear. First, the rate of publishing has climbed steadily, dramatically increasing the number of printed pieces to be acquired, processed, housed, and circulated by libraries. Second, a rapidly expanding and more literate population has generated demands for readers services that have far exceeded a library's ability to respond effectively with traditional methods and techniques. Third, the library as a "labor intensive" operation, heavily dependent on manpower, is faced with significant problems in its budget as salaries and wages steadily increase. Fourth, the continuing improvement in the qualitative characteristics and economic efficiency of available technology has finally made mechanized solutions to these problems feasible. Prospects for the future suggest that these factors will become increasingly significant. Hence, professional librarians, like other administrators, have been prompted to look for help to the new technology available in modern data processing equipment and systems. (151:4)

The effect of technological development is emphasized by Hayes's description of the Yale University experience:

> Yale University took a somewhat different approach to mechanization. Starting with the acquisitions procedures at Yale Medical Library, under the direction of

Fred Kilgour, they experimented in 1963 with the use of machine based cataloging data. An experimental project was inaugurated involving Yale, Harvard and Columbia in a sharing of cataloging data. However, the project *was in advance of the technological capabilities . . . at the time.* (Emphasis added.) (151:54)

The importance of technological capability is indicated by subsequent developments at the Ohio College Library Center, also directed by Fred Kilgour. This center began only four years after the Yale experiments, but the improvements in technology combined with experience in operating such systems has led to the development of one of the major networks in the United States. (151:54)

While this one representative sample does not tell the whole story, it becomes clear that the two elements that aid in achieving improved systems are technological systems and creative innovators. The efforts of Parker, Fairthorne, Shera, Perry, Vickery, Kent, Hayes, Leimkuhler, Becker, Kilgour Buckland, MacKenzie, and many others pushed the designs for systems beyond the capabilities of the machine. This lead the manufacturers to further efforts in refining equipment to meet the new demands. The interacting process between practitioner and the equipment designer creates the potential for successively more sophisticated capability and more sophisticated applications.

By 1975, the developments in computer technology had completely changed the information processing environment. The computer that was available in 1960 was card-oriented, required extensive operator intervention, and used more of its available power on input–output tasks than on processing tasks. By the end of the decade, tape- and disc-oriented computers had been integrated by supervisory operating systems that focused the equipment on the primary processing functions. These developments paved the way for the interactive systems which have emerged as the mainstream of processing technology. The trend has been accelerated by the emergence of the minicomputer and the microprocessor.

The minicomputer brings the computer within scale for small operations which did not require and could not afford the massive systems that were developed in the 1960s. These computers have the ability to store extensive, but not massive, files, perform all the standard operations of the larger computers, and, most importantly, communicate with the larger machines. This makes it possible to utilize equipment appropriate for the functions which need to be accomplished. The minicomputer serves the needs of the intermediate operations which are large enough to require the electronic processing capability but too small to require the full-scale installation of a major computer. The microprocessor extends this concept to even smaller operations.

The microprocessor has less capability for processing at the local site than the minicomputer. It serves primarily as a data collection and transmission device, but it accomplishes these tasks in an automatic mode. With the availability of the micropressor, the computer processing environment changes again, and, as a result, extends the number of organizations which can apply electronic processing to its operations.

As computers continue to evolve, what changes appear probable in future library applications?

There are four major factors that will influence the future application of computers in libraries: attitudes, management systems, telecommunications, and computer technology. The attitudes of librarians and the management systems to coordinate the elements of national networks into operating systems represent the people elements in systems design. These will be the most difficult parts of the system to create. The telecommunication component is partly a people (political) problem, partly a technological problem, and partly an economic problem. The dominant corporation has a virtual monopoly of telephone services in the United States. This means that it will be necessary to resolve the political and economic aspects of data communication in order to achieve significant changes in the telecommunications environment. How this can be resolved is still difficult to perceive. Small steps have been taken to open the field to alternative communication systems. This will have the effect of encouraging research and development activities as well as efforts to devise new structures to provide telecommunications services.

The management systems are gradually being evolved through the work of the National Commission on Library and Information Services, but the progress is slow because these are situations that are new to our society. The national corporation is relatively common, but the concept of a national service system with both public and private components is much less common. The task is to resolve the dynamic tension produced by the need to make knowledge accessible to all and the desire for a profit-making entity which will relieve some of the burden on public funding. Of all the elements involved, the computer technology is the one which advances most rapidly and the one we wish to address.

Within the area of computer technology, there are three developments which will contribute to library computer applications in the future: the refinement of data collection methods, the application of the minicomputer, and the applications of microprocessors in library systems. A fourth element will accelerate the development of library systems in the future, but it is the result of expanding operations rather than technology. This is the rapidly expanding data bases of bibliographic information that are becoming available in machine readable form. The effect of these data bases will be to reduce the cost of converting from manual to machine readable files and, consequently, the start-up costs for library computer systems. For our purposes in this chapter, emphasis will be concentrated on the computer developments.

Three significant developments in computer technology have been noted. Our discussion of these probable developments must be viewed against the large-scale computer which stands behind these more recent developments. It is not likely that refinements in design and architecture of large-scale computers will stop with the present equipment configurations. The central processing units, input-output devices, and storage devices will continue to improve in operating speeds, storage densities, and interaction speeds.

The developments in minicomputers and microprocessors must be seen in relation to these backup systems which support major systems using the smaller devices for local operations. These local units combined with data collection systems provide the means of expanding library applications to library situations which were previously uneconomic.

The problem of data collection has impeded many computer applications in the past. The task of keyboarding every item of information made many installations slow and mitigated the advantages of the high processing speeds of the computer. The charge plate type of identification card punched with Hollerith code characters has been available for many years, but has not had efficient supporting equipment. Several circulation systems have been designed around early versions of IBM data collection devices. Present designs of these devices show promise for circulation systems in libraries. Recent developments with bar coded labels and light pens have also improved the data collection operations in simplicity, speed, and equipment costs.

Bar coded labels are white labels with a series of black lines which can be "read" by a light pen. The line represents numeric codes which the light pen translates into electronic impulses and records on magnetic tape or transmits to a microprocessor. This device provides an important component for library circulation systems because it provides a compact device that can be located at the circulation service points, is inexpensive to duplicate for several service points and is integrated into systems based on minicomputers and microprocessors. These small-scale computers are the important components in recently developed library circulation control systems.

The minicomputer has made library applications feasible for medium size library situations. It has storage capacities which meet the library needs for files and the processing capabilities to handle the library routines. The major files used so far are bibliographic data bases representing the library's collection and the borrowers file. These are used to generate the circulation transaction files. Telecommunication features permit intermediate levels of processing to be completed at the local library site while larger processing tasks are completed in large-scale computers at remote locations in machine-to-machine communication modes. When these features are combined with the shared cost of programming support, the minicomputer becomes a powerful tool at reasonable cost.

The microprocessor extends these cost advantages to smaller libraries. It is an extremely compact device with a medium range of processing power and intermediate levels of storage capacity. Standardized transaction routines are preprogrammed and the file capacity is large enough to handle the volume of daily transactions. Automatic machine-to-machine communication with remote large-scale computers provides for integrating each day's circulation transactions into large files maintained at the remote location. Many of the processing functions are carried on in the remote location—for example, producing overdue notices in the Gaylord system. This relieves the library staff of handling many of the overdue routines in the local library since notices can be mailed back to the library in bulk or mailed directly to the borrower from the computing facility.

The effect of the microprocessor will be to automate many library routines at higher levels of machine capability with fewer occasions when human intervention is required. This increases the speed at which routines can be completed. With the relatively low need for computer knowledge and competency, libraries with smaller staffs do not need to train or to hire someone to handle extensive computer tasks.

As microprocessors become more widely available, the potential for a genuine national library network comes closer to reality. Assuming that bibliographic record formats are standardized, that processing languages are standardized, and that telecommunciation facilities are standardized, the probable future applications of computers in libraries will be combinations of microprocessors in very small libraries, minicomputers at type of library or subject library clusters, and large-scale computer capacity at regional centers. At the present time, it is expected that several levels of regional centers will emerge: states and clusters of states. In addition to these networks of general libraries, the national centers will also emerge, for example, Spires-Ballots, OCLC, the National Library of Medicine, etc. The prospect is a system in which any bibliographic item can be identified and located automatically by machine-to-machine communications. Human intervention will be needed to reproduce the item or to retrieve and mail it to the requestor. It is likely that some automatic recording system will identify the use of the item and assess a charge for its use which will be paid to the copyright holder of the item.

Selected Readings

Artandi, Susan. 1972. *An introduction to computers in information science.* 2d ed. Metuchen, N.J.: Scarecrow.

Hayes, Robert M., and Becker, Joseph. 1974. Processing of data. In *Handbook of data processing for libraries,* pp. 237–76. 2d ed. Los Angeles: Melville.

Hughes, John L. 1968. *Digital computer lab workbook.* Maynard, Mass.: Digital Equipment Corporation.

International Business Machines. 1970. *Special academic computer concepts course for university, library, and museum executives and scholarly associations in the humanities.* 2d ed. White Plains, N.Y.

Kelly, William F. 1969. Automatic data processing—electronic data processing. In *Management through systems and procedures: the total systems concept,* pp. 417–72. New York: Wiley.

U.S. Atomic Energy Commission. Division of Technical Information. 1968. *Computers.* Oak Ridge, Tenn.

Van Amerongen, C. 1974. *The way things work, book of the computer: an illustrated encyclopedia of information science, cybernetics, and data processing.* New York: Simon and Schuster.

7. Programming languages

The development of the computer would be insignificant were it not for parallel developments in the field of programming languages. It is the programming language which makes it possible to communicate with the computer and give it the instructions it must follow to complete a job. The time and expense of computer applications is greatly affected by programming costs. As languages have evolved, these costs are being reduced in two ways: by the sale of programs, relieving the need for rewriting standard programs in every installation, and by the use of higher level languages to simplify the programming task.

The development of programming languages parallels the development of the computer in some respects. The essential trend has been to transfer as much of the detailed work as possible to the computer through the use of standardized "languages." These languages actually make use of programs which translate instructions from the programmer into machine language operating instructions; computers operate only on machine language codes in binary or hexadecimal numbers. In the early computers, the programmer wrote out ten-digit numbers which include the operating code, the location of the first operand, and the location of the second operand. A typical instruction would appear as 2109510220 where 21 is an add instruction, 0951 is the location of the first number, and 0220 is the location of the second number. The complete instruction tells the machine to add the number in location 0951 to the number in 0220 and store the result in 0220. Since every time the data is moved, operated on, or stored a new instruction is required, it is apparent that the programming is not only tedious but also subject to error.

Experience with programming showed that many programs used the same sequences of steps in accomplishing particular tasks. It was a short step from that knowledge to the development of programming languages in which specified statements were used to generate a series of machine language commands to the computer. Two types of languages came from this early experience: assembly languages and compiler languages. In an assembly language, the programmer instructions begin to approximate statements in abbreviated English and there is a direct transformation from an assembly language statement into a machine language statement. Compiler languages become more complex. A programming language statement usually generates a series of machine language statements in the form of a standardized subroutine. One of the earliest compiler or higher level languages is FORTRAN, in which an approximation of mathematical expressions (limited by the available character sets on key punch machines) are transformed into a series of machine language statements carrying out the operations defined in the mathematical expression.

Another early language is COBOL, designed for computer applications in business operations. In COBOL (Common Business Oriented Language), English language statements are used to write the program. The program is arranged in three divisions, which handle data designations and files, housekeeping operations, and the operating instructions of the program. Both of these languages are compiler languages, and because of their popularity are available on most computing systems.

From this early development in programming languages, a number of more sophisticated languages have been devised. Some, e.g., PL/1 produced by IBM for its 360 and 370 series computers, are general purpose languages capable of being used for any type of application. Others, e.g., GPSS, SIMSCRIPT, and SNOBOL, are specialized languages used for particular applications. GPSS, General Purpose Systems Simulator, is a specialized language used in computer simulation. SIMSCRIPT is another simulation language developed by the Rand Corporation in Santa Monica, California. SNOBOL is a string transformation language which some individuals advocate for library programming use.

Each programming language reflects the philosophy and purpose of the language originator. FORTRAN was designed by IBM for use in solving mathematical problems. While it has been used in library applications, it is not the language best suited for library programming. COBOL, which was designed as a result of user demand and federal government effort, is directed toward commercial data processing and reflects the needs of business, financial, and accounting data processing needs.

The characteristics of library applications differ from most other types of data-processing activities. The files are primarily alphabetic rather than numeric. Except for a relatively small amount of business processing in accounting procedures, most of the tasks are sorting, merging, collating, or comparing, and usually these operations are performed on very large files. The typical library record consisting of bibliographic and user data tends to be larger than typical business records and less easily standardized in terms of the number of characters. The use of computers in sorting large files in alphabetical sequence is more complicated in library applications because of the filing rules needed for bibliographic records.

These characteristics of library processing requirements make it necessary to consider programming languages with care. It is usually possible to program any activity in any general purpose programming language. The results may be poor, however, because of the inefficient ways in which certain tasks must be accomplished. It is possible that as the volume of library data processing increases, a specialized language will be developed. The development of such a language requires some understanding of the differences that distinguish programming languages from ordinary languages.

In what way are programming languages
different from ordinary languages?

Programming languages differ from ordinary languages in important aspects: the function of the language and the restraints on the language. These affect the application of computers in particular situations.

The function of the programming language is to facilitate the use of the computer. The computer is designed with a set of operations built into the machine. These operations are initiated by instructions interpreted by the computer from punched cards, magnetic tapes and discs, or internal machine storage. The instructions must be recorded in some form of coding, usually binary, which can be recorded in ways the equipment can detect by mechanical means (punched tape and punched cards) or by electronic means (magnetic media). Some set of instructions must be combined to direct the machine to perform each step in any task that the machine is being used to accomplish. The instructions move data (including instructions), perform arithmetic and logical operations, store data, compare, etc. Since many jobs are repeated frequently in standard operations, the instructions can be combined into subroutines. Programming languages are symbolic representations for single instructions or subroutines which make it possible to combine series of subroutines into processing tasks. The number of instructions and subroutines is limited, however, and it is easier to understand these limits by reviewing the restraints as they occur in the major categories of programming languages: assembly languages and compiler languages.

Assembly languages are the most flexible and the most

extensive languages. They are designed to simplify the task of the programmer by providing mnemonic devices and "symbolic" addressing features. As Palmer points out:

It is possible to write programs in machine language, but extremely laborious if they are of any substantive size. The difficulty is not so much because the machine operation codes frequently lack mnemonic qualities, or even because of the often difficult address notation, but because of the problem of keeping an absolutely precise count of positions used and knowing the machine location of every instruction and every other item which must be referred to. . . . (262:201).

The programmer uses assembly language to write a source program. This program is translated into an object program by a special program known as an assembly program. The defined terms, punctuation and symbols of the assembly language are interpreted by the computer and translated into a machine language program which can be loaded into the computer from punched cards, magnetic tape, or discs. A statement in the assembly language usually translates into a single machine instruction. By combining individual instructions into sets of instructions called macros, the assembly language allows the programmer to refer to frequently used sequences of instructions by a single statement. This adds to the facility with which programs can be written; the task still requires long lists of instructions to prepare a program. The terms that can be used in the assembly language are strictly defined, and the kind of statements that can be made is limited by the design of the assembly program. These restraints have made it necessary for the programmmer to know the equipment very well and to understand the programming language very well. Training programmers requires many hours of instruction and experience, while programming costs often have become prohibitive. To alleviate this difficulty, higher level languages have been designed in which statements represent one or more macros. These languages begin to approximate statements and symbol combinations that are familiar to people and consequently easier to use.

The higher level languages—FORTRAN, COBOL, ALGOL, etc.—provide many more terms and much more flexibility for the programmer because much of the work is transferred to the machine. The programmer works with mathematical notation, modified to fit the character sets of the computer, as in FORTRAN, or with English statements, as in COBOL. The restraints remain, however, and only specifically designated words are admitted and sometimes only under limited conditions. These statements are transformed into a machine language program by a compiler program. This program, unlike the assembler program, uses a single programming language statement to generate strings of machine instructions. The restraints on terms, combinations of terms, and statement in early compiler or higher level languages still required extensive training in the language before a usable level of competence could be achieved. This difficulty has been resolved by the development of modular forms of compiler languages.

The modular concept in programming languages makes the computer still more accessible to the average user. By redesigning or modifying the programming languages so that usable knowledge of the language can be acquired with a few hours of instruction and experience, the user can begin to apply the computer to his particular problems more quickly. As he gains proficiency with the language, he can begin to develop programs of greater complexity and use the computer to solve more significant problems in his particular area of interest. It is the application that plays an important role in the language a particular user will find most valuable. Our concern with libraries and library applications leads us to consider the applicability of programming languages to library processing operations.

What languages are most useful in library applications and what characteristics do these languages share?

The immediately apparent characteristics of library computer applications are the need for large files, the capability of processing large alphanumeric records, and, for most purposes, relatively modest computational power. The list can be extended to include logical operations and operations involving matching, comparing, etc. Languages such as FORTRAN and ALGOL are algorithmic and are designed primarily for computation. These languages provide conventions for translating standard mathematical formulas into the machine character sets. Early computers had limited character sets and alternatives to standard notation had to be found. Exponentiation, for example, is indicated in FORTRAN and other languages by ** rather than by superscript characters, which are unavailable in computers and earlier key punches. The early emphasis on scientific applications prompted the need for programming languages which could be used by the scientist to solve complex mathematical problems. As the application of computers extended to business, the need for nonmathematically oriented languages became evident. One of the earliest of these is COBOL.

COBOL was designed for business applications. It uses plain language phrases and familiar terminology, e.g., create file, etc. The terminology and phrases are typical of the needs in business processing applications. Concurrently with these developments, manufacturers and computer users have designed a number of languages with particular characteristics. Each represents some important need for a particular group of users and serves the same function as FORTRAN and COBOL, namely, to facilitate programming for specific applications.

Hayes provides a short list of the most important languages that have been developed to date (151:264-65). The probable future trend will be refinements of PL/1, which was developed by IBM and combines the best features of FORTRAN and COBOL. It combines algorithmic and plain language statements characteristic of these two languages. PL/1 is based on the modular concept and provides a basic concept that will continue to be valuable for both batch processing and on-line applications.

The languages most appropriate for library applications

are those which provide efficient sorting routines, the ability to handle variable length records in alphanumeric characters, provisions for file maintenance functions, and simplicity in learning and in use. Library applications have been programmed in FORTRAN, COBOL, SNOBOL, FLIRT (A proprietary language of CLSI), and many others. Most frequently, the programming language is determined by the type of equipment and the kind of programming support available from the computing facility that is used for the applications. The problem of programming support is one with which librarians can easily sympathize, for it has analogies in the support of classification systems. Without ongoing reevaluation of the languages, the modifications needed are not incorporated into the language to meet new needs in applications. When continuing support is available, as in manufacturer supported languages, there is a continuous revision and refinement of the language, increasing its flexibility, extending the range of statements, and simplifying procedures for its use.

Programming languages are being continually refined to reduce the time and effort of the programmer in developing a program package for a specific application. Combined with the rapidly emerging packaged programs, which perform a number of standard routines, it is becoming relatively easy for the library to begin applying computers to its basic operations. The perennial questions of cost versus benefit remain. We shall see in the next chapter that while no immediate breakthroughs are imminent, there is a steady progress being made in the applications of computers to the requirements of library information handling.

Selected Readings

Brophy, Peter. *Cobol Programming: An Introduction for librarians,* London, Bingley; Hamden, Ct., Linnet Books.
Davis, Charles H. 1974. *Illustrative computer programming*

for libraries: selected examples for information specialists. Westport, Conn.: Greenwood Press.

Dodd, K. N. 1969. Computer programming and languages. New York: Plenum Press.

Elson, Mark. 1973. Introduction to programming languages. In Concepts of programming languages, pp. 1-63. Chicago: Science Research Associates.

George, F. H. 1968. An introduction to computer programming. London: Pergamon.

Hayes, Robert M., and Becker, Joseph. 1974. Processing of data. In Handbook of data processing for libraries, pp. 255-76.

Katzan, H. 1973. Introduction to programming languages. Philadelphia: Auerbach Publishers, Inc.

Palmer, F. M. 1968. Computer programming for the librarian. Drexel library quarterly 4:197-213.

8. Library automation

The library's function in contemporary society is to serve as the access point for knowledge and to serve as the memory bank for man's recorded knowledge. Librarians caught up in the day-to-day needs of the local situation recognize the value of the knowledge that is contained in their collections, but they have frequently failed to communicate the value of knowledge to those outside the library. The use of automation in libraries must be seen from two perspectives: the user's need for knowledge, and the cost of retrieving knowledge from large files.

Systems analysis contributes to improved productivity so that the cost of retrieving knowledge is reduced. It must also be viewed in terms of future potential. The technological capability to create library networks and bibliographic information centers exists. The task now is to find the means of funding these activities and reaching beyond the limitations of bibliographic information. The user needs knowledge. To provide knowledge to the user is the library's long-range goal, and it becomes necessary in our present discussion of the goal to look at the capabilities of knowledge retrieval rather than bibliographic data retrieval. In this chapter, however, we examine some of the standard subsystems in the library and the present efforts to apply computers to these subsystems. Our exploration will consider both the application in individual libraries and the use of library network systems that use the telecommunications capabilities of the computer.

While several early applications of punched card equipment were made in library operations, the significant use of mechanization has had to depend on technological developments which were consistent with the needs of library data processing. These developments included the capability to manipulate alphabetic data efficiently, storage capacity sufficient to store extremely large files, and, to a lesser degree, typefaces that provided more elegant output than that needed in most commercial data processing. It took approximately ten years, from 1954 to 1964, before these refinements in computers became readily available.

Experimentation did not stop because of the limitations, however, and considerable progress was made prior to 1964. With the advent of tape oriented computers and the development of operating systems capable of monitoring the large-scale computer, effective development of library systems accelerated. In analyzing library operations, it is common to divide the library into a set of six subsystems: administration, circulation, acquisitions, cataloging and classification, serial records, and reference. Library administrators, mediating need and resources, have approached library automation from a number of positions. A few have emphasized the use of computers in management information systems, more have approached the problem from the needs of cataloging or acquisitions, and many have begun with circulation control. These approaches are consistent with the principles of systems analysis and the concepts of computer applications. Generally, the librarians have viewed the library as a total system and recognized the limitations of their resources. As a result of the need to focus on the most productive applications, attention turned first to circulation because of the volume of processing, to cataloging because of the costs associated with catalog production and maintenance, and to acquisitions because of the combination of similiarities to purchasing activities in other types of organizations and the application of accounting procedures to maintain control of budget allocations, and, finally, to serial records systems because of the recurring nature of posting the receipt of current issues and the perodic renewal of subscriptions. The least effort has been directed to applications in reference. This function of the library is comparable to information retrieval systems and in terms of costs, in most libraries does not loom as large as other activities. Furthermore, the auto-mation of the reference function represents one of the more complex applications of computers, which means high costs for relatively low immediate benefit. The result of much library automation has been local in origin and local in application. At least three of these local systems have emerged as potential network systems: Spires-Ballots, Ohio College Library Center (OCLC), and CLSI's Libs 100.

Spires-Ballots began as an acquisitions and cataloging system in the Stanford University Libraries. Some of its features, particularly the KWIC indexing elements, have made it more generally useful as a means of identifying and locating cataloging information. Through a time-sharing system, the Spires-Ballots system is now available to a num-ber of users within the state of California and in other loca-tions. The Ohio College Library Center had similar origins. It began as a centralized system for delivering catalog copy to the independent colleges in Ohio. As the system has been perfected and the telecommunications facilities became available, libraries throughout the country have found it ad-vantageous to obtain cataloging copy from this file, which rapidly increases its usefulness as it accumulates input from MARC tapes and from the participating libraries.

CLSI began as a private commercial firm offering a num-ber of program packages in a turnkey system specifically designed to handle library information handling needs. The basic system uses minicomputers located in the user libraries with associated CRT/Keyboard terminals and light pen data collection devices for recording circulation. The main compu-ter is located in Newburyport, Massachusetts, with the user library linked by telephone. The system automatically records loan transactions and returns, prepares overdue notices, and accumulates records of unpaid fines, lost book charges, and other items of information relating to circulation transactions.

These systems are not true networks. They have the potential of becoming the nuclei of national networks which may eventually link clusters of libraries in various geographical regions into a network arrangement. As equipment costs for storage and computation continue to decrease in terms of cost per unit of storage or cost per computation and as telecommunication costs are improved, the use of remote computers even across the transcontinental United States becomes more economical in relation to local processing.

What are the basic elements of an automated library system?

An automated library system differs from other systems only in the kind of files maintained, and even these bear similarities to other applications. The basic elements of data processing systems include: record formats, input-output processing procedures, specifications, processing operations (transformations), and system documentation. Each of these contributes to the operation of the system in different ways and their contribution can be seen from an explanation of these elements.

The record format is the fundamental element from which the system is developed. Systems are designed and operated to provide access to information and the information is normally contained in some descriptive record. The familiar catalog card is an example of a record. In machine systems, the definition of the record is much more critical because the machine is unable to make allowances for minor discrepancies which people handle without difficulty. The record format is defined in terms of fields and characters. The fields indicate the kind of information that will be recorded and have an associated code that provides an unambiguous identification of the field. Fields are designated "fixed" or "variable" according to their specification: fixed fields have a defined number of characters; variable fields are assigned a maximum number of characters and may have from zero to the maximum number of characters. Variable fields also require a character count subfield so that the field can be moved and manipulated.

Record formats are used first in the input operations which indicate how data will be introduced into the system. In a library system, this is most often a bibliographic record which will be added to the library's data base. As records are accumulated, they are added to the files which form the data base and are used for subsequent processing to obtain the outputs for which the system is designed.

Several files will normally be required, and these depend on the system objectives. The major file will be the master file of the library's data base. The master file is stored on magnetic tape or on discs in the ways which makes processing most efficient for the subsequent processing tasks that are required. File management becomes an extremely important concern in batch processing operations using magnetic tapes; the characteristics of disk storage relax some of the restraints imposed by sequential tape files. The master file will be supplemented by subsidiary files and will include one or more of the following: current transaction files, address files, and, in libraries, authority files, etc. Current transaction files will record each day's transactions. At regular intervals, the transaction file will be merged with the master file to provide an updated master file. Address files and other supplementary files will be maintained by steps in the processing cycle. Once the file is created these transactions occur infrequently, depending on the nature of the system. The files are now ready for use in the processing operations and the type of system will determine the frequency and kinds of operations that are used.

Each system is designed to accomplish certain objectives. These objectives are usually specified in terms of outputs from the system. Some outputs are obtained in order to serve a later function of the system and are subsequently transformed still further to produce the final output. The specification of output is critical in the design of the system, and, for most systems, this is the first element designed. Once the output form and format, e.g., tape files, disk files, computer output on microfilm (COM), etc., has been selected, the system is designed by determining the necessary prior steps that will produce the intended output.

These four elements constitute the basics of the data processing system. They vary in some degree according to whether a batch processing or on-line mode of operation will be used, but they are found in every system.

What are some of the library subsystems
that lend themselves most readily to computer applications?

Several factors are analyzed when data-processing applications are considered in any organization. These factors must also be evaluated in library applications of computers. The two most important factors are: volume of transactions and complexity of the task. When little volume is involved, it is usually not economic to use computers in the operation. Volume may be measured in frequency or in total number of transactions and is taken into consideration when systems are studied. Complexity of a task may require a number of detailed analyses to determine whether or not a computer is necessary. Normally, library operations that lend themselves to automation include both volume and complexity with low levels of computational power. When we examine the library as a total system, we find several subsystems within it which lend themselves to computer applications.

The most obvious subsystem in the library that demands mechanization is the circulation system. This file usually accounts for the most transactions during a day or year, and each transaction can become complex, although the standard transaction requires simple data transcription. The total number of man-hours devoted to circulation control in most libraries suggests this as a productive place to begin automation.

The next most active operation in the library will probably be either serial records activities or acquisitions activities.

Both require a high volume of transactions, with a combination of logical and arithmetic operations, and continuing follow-up to keep all of the transactions under control. The important element in most of the library systems is the dependence on large files of bibliographic data. This leads to the fourth subsystem: cataloging and classification. The volume of transactions in cataloging and classification is comparable to the level of serial acquisitions and separates (monograph) acquisitions combined when serials are fully cataloged. The task becomes more complex in libraries because of the demand for consistent entries, the use of authority files for entries and for subject headings, and the need to revise these subsidiary files to keep them current. Additional complexities are introduced by the demands of filing rules to meet the needs of large files and other characteristics of the library catalog. These elements are being revised currently to incorporate the modifications needed to standardize entries for bibliographic items at the international level while taking advantage of the machine processing capabilities.

The last library system we can identify is the reference system. This has received the least effort in some respects although it was the first in need. Information retrieval systems such as MEDLARS and others demonstrated the capabilities of machine literature searching. The staff of the Documentation Institute at Case Western Reserve were forerunners in some of the notable information storage and retrieval projects. These projects provided the knowledge and experience that have enabled us to improve such services continuously. At the present time, the economic resources are not available to design and implement reference retrieval systems at the library level. They have been designed as commercial ventures or as professional information retrieval systems such as *Chemical Abstracts*.

This discussion of library automation suggests some of the elements in library data processing systems and the subsystems of the library which lend themselves to computer applications. They do not exhaust the applications that have been made in libraries, but simply indicate the potential this equipment holds for libraries and information systems. At the same time, it suggests the urgent need to begin exploring the more complex elements of library services, particularly the reference and research functions. These must be extended beyond the present attempts to find bibliographic data retrieval systems that facilitate the technical work of the library to retrieval systems that aid the user in getting the functional knowledge he needs.

Selected Readings

Alper, Bruce H. 1975. Library automation. In *Annual review of information science and technology,* vol. 10. Washington, D.C.

Bernstein, H. H. 1971. Some organizational prerequisites for the introduction of electronic data processing in libraries. *Libri* 21:15-25.

Carter, Ruth C. 1973. Systems analysis as a prelude to library automation. *Library trends* 21:505-21.

Chapman, Edward A., St. Pierre, Paul L., and Lubans, John, 1970. Principles of systems design. In *Library systems analysis guidelines,* pp. 112-51. New York: Wiley.

Delanoy, Diana. 1975. Technology: present status and trends in computers. In *Library automation: state of the art II,* ed. Susan K. Martin and Brett Butler, pp. 18-37. Chicago: ALA.

Fasana, Paul J. 1967. Determining the cost of library automation. *ALA Bulletin* 61:656-61.

International Business Machines. 1972. *Library automation—introduction to data processing.* White Plains, N.Y.

Kilgour, Frederick G. 1970. History of library computerization. *Journal of library automation* 62:117-24.

Landau, Herbert. 1971. Can the librarian become a computer data base manager? *Special libraries* 62:117-24.

Markuson, Barbara E., et al. 1972. Library automation guidelines. In *Guidelines for library automation: a handbook for federal and other libraries,* pp. 6-18. Santa Monica, Calif.: System Development Corporation.

Markuson, Barbara E. 1970. An overview of library automation. *Datamation* 16:60-68.

Mather, Dan. 1968. Data processing in an academic library: some conclusions and observations. *PNLA quarterly* 32:4-21.

Salton, Gerard. 1975. Mechanized housekeeping. In *Dynamic information and library processing*, pp. 39-75. Englewood Cliffs, N.J.: Prentice-Hall.

Shoffner, Ralph M. 1975. Outlook for the future. In *Library automation: state of the art II*, ed. Susan K. Martin and Brett Butler, pp. 1-17. Chicago: ALA.

Veaner, B. Allen. 1971. Approaches to library automation. *Law library journal* 64:146-53.

———. 1975. Perspective: review of 1968-1973 in library automation. In *Library automation state of the art II*, ed. Susan K. Martin and Brett Butler, pp. 1-17. Chicago: ALA.

9. Cost studies

The cost of library operations becomes increasingly important as the trend to program budgeting continues and as
budget authorities become more concerned with productivity.
In systems work, the typical study of costs centers around the
present and the proposed methods of performing a particular
task. For management purposes, the most effective cost information comes from a continuing cost accounting system.
Both of these functions—cost comparison and cost control—
are related. Since sound systems work would require the
development of control systems to monitor and evaluate new
methods in operation, the development of a cost accounting
system can be considered a part of the system study objective.
For our purposes, it will be useful to examine the cost accounting approach to cost control and then to consider these elements in the comparison of costs for proposed systems.

Cost accounting is a management tool which, through
periodic reports, provides current and historical cost information. When a cost accounting system is initiated, it provides
only current information; as data accumulates in the system,
it provides comparative data for the current reporting period,

the previous period, and usually the same period in the previous fiscal year. Other alternatives are possible and the content of the report is determined by management needs.

Cost accounting reports are summaries of operating data. The goal is to synthesize the data so that operating results can be displayed as clearly and as simply as possible. The usual form of cost accounting reports presents data as "unit costs." This is the cost of producing one completed standard unit of work, e.g., cataloging a monograph, cataloging a pamphlet, etc. This is the most detailed level of cost. Two levels of cost data may be used for cost accounting reports: process costs and job costs. Each of these levels may be reported in terms of direct costs or total costs.

Process costs represent the cost of an activity. It can be, for example, the cost of processing purchase orders, the cost of acquisitions (as a process, not as cost per volume), or the cost of technical services functions. Each represents a level of detail in the cost-accounting system ranging from the work group to the section or department. Job costs represent the cost of writing a single purchase order, acquiring a single publication, or completing all the processing of each item worked on in a technical services procedure. Each of these costs can be based on direct costs, meaning the cost of labor, supplies, and equipment, or on total costs, meaning the direct costs plus a proportionate part of the costs of administration, building, and maintenance. These latter items are indirect costs. The distribution of indirect costs is never simple and the basis on which the distribution is made can have important ramifications on the overall cost picture of operations. We gain some appreciation of the difficulties in our first question on unit costs.

What is a unit cost and how do you arrive at it?

The unit cost is a "typical rate for handling a single unit" (151:119). As Hayes points out, the problem is more complex than it appears because of the difficulty of allocating indirect costs to a task. Ideally, we would like to have cost data which is comparable over time within the same library operation as well as comparable to data available from other libraries. The first will indicate changes in operations within the library; the second provides comparisons with similar libraries.

The simplest cost figure is the "basic cost unit" which Hayes defines as " . . . the cost one would expect to find as direct costs (per unit of work) reported by a cost accounting system. They are therefore the average cost per unit of work including nonproductive time (such as coffee breaks), inefficiencies, and variations in work load." (151:120.)

More refined versions of the unit are "standard cost," and "burdened cost." The standard cost includes allowance for personnel benefits, e.g., vacations, holidays, sick leaves, etc. (151:120). Although they are not mentioned by Hayes, the basic and standard costs may also include equipment and supply costs, e.g., the cost of copying cards, the cost of multi-part order forms, etc. It should also be noted that standard costs are normally derived from the use of time studies to find the time for typical rates of production rather than those which might vary because of differences in work load.

The burdened cost represents the combination of direct costs for labor, supplies, equipment, and personnel benefits as well as a distribution of overhead costs which include supervision, utilities, maintenance, etc. These costs form a substantial cost of operations and must be distributed in some way over the different activities which are part of the library. While they appear to be the same in all libraries, the particular accounting practices will lead to different results and we now address this aspect of unit costs.

What difficulties appear to cause the disparity in the results of published cost studies?

At each level in the cost analysis process different factors contribute to variations in cost study results. The first difficulty occurs in the details of the activity. Many libraries use the same terms to describe different operations. Preacquisition searching, for example, may simply mean a search through catalogs and process files to determine that the title is not yet on order, or it may mean a detailed bibliographic verification of the record together with a recording of appropriate cataloging data to be forwarded to the cataloging department. Costs for these two activities will differ greatly, but the difference in costs must be compared in terms of results achieved. The first method means that many of the steps must be repeated by the cataloging department and these costs must be included to make meaningful comparisons with the results of the second method.

The second major variation in library costs will occur at the level of burdened costs. The method used to distribute supervisory costs, space, utilities, maintenance, and other operating costs must be the same to make valid comparisons between libraries. The advantage of interlibrary comparison is the ability to determine efficient methods. The cost studies simply provide information relating to methods; other methods must be used to determine effectiveness and these are often unique to the individual institution. The significant value of cost studies, however, comes from comparisons between present and past performance. It is this function of cost studies that we consider next.

How can cost studies contribute to improved library services?

The primary purpose of cost studies is to evaluate the way a particular library allocates its resources and the benefits it derives from this allocation. This becomes an integral part of systems analysis and design, for the effective design incorporates subsystems which provide feedback and evaluation data. While costs are not the only measures of effective operations, there is a relationship between costs (or time) and performance in many activities. These become apparent under examination and after the analysis of costs. For example, the time required to process documents represents one measure of efficiency—how well the task is performed—when defined standards of quality control are imposed on the process. Above and beyond the simple matter of efficiency, the decrease in time from receipt to availability for use, for example, represents a measure of effectiveness, for it makes the publications more available to the user. Other measures must be used to determine the relevance of the documents to the users' needs, but this does not preclude the speed of processing as a measure of effectiveness.

When we refer to improved library services, we make a number of statements: we wish to make more documents available, we wish to interpose as few barriers to effective use as possible, we wish to keep the operating costs as low as possible and divert funds to more effective collections, and we want these publications to be available as soon after their appearance as possible. Not all of these qualifiers are measurable. We can readily identify more documents by a simple count; it is not easy to identify or measure "more relevant to users' needs." Similarly, the means of measuring index effectiveness is very limited, but the speed with which documents are made available can be plotted without difficulty.

It is partly because of the ease of measuring (or counting) some elements of the system that we have collected the kinds of statistics usually presented by libraries. Often, however, these are intermediate measures and the need is to develop more sensitive measures of the value of the service to the user—an intangible element of library services. As cost studies continue, however, we can improve the mechanics of the system; the next stage is to improve the quality of the service through continuing systems studies.

It should be apparent that cost accounting is itself an activity which entails a cost for the library. The level of detail that is used will be made on the basis of the value received for the costs entailed. For most practical situations, it would be sufficient to maintain a system of reporting processing costs. Where performance budgeting is used, however, many authorities require job costs based on group performance. The typical procedure is to ignore supply and equipment costs and to focus on labor costs. The data on labor costs for the operational unit or activity is then related to the output of the unit which are shown by the statistics regularly collected in libraries, e.g., titles cataloged, etc.

The procedure that can be followed effectively is to develop an activity or funtional organization chart showing the number and level of employees engaged in each activity and the regularly scheduled hours. When variations occur as a result of absence for any reason, the hours lost (or scheduled out) are recorded. These include: illness, personal business, vacation, reassignment, etc. The purpose is to record only the deviations from the expected scheduling. The losses are subtracted from the scheduled hours to provide the actual hours worked for the activity or unit. The production statistics are then related to the hours worked to obtain a production rate in units per hour or time per unit. This is a gross measure of costs because the cost is based on average hourly labor costs. For more precise measures, it is necessary to elaborate on the record-keeping system to establish the number of hours at each hourly rate and equate these hourly rates to the unit produced.

The value of a cost-accounting system lies in its potential as a means of controlling costs at every level of operations. At the supervisory level, the cost data provides a means of evaluating the minor changes in procedures that are made on an *ad hoc* basis in the day-to-day work situation. Summarized at successively higher levels of operation, the cost-reporting system provides the department head and the administration with a good view of the way the total system is functioning. Finally, the accumulation of cost data becomes valuable for the systems study in which proposed costs must be compared with the costs of the existing system.

One of the objectives of the system study is the development of methods which will improve costs in one of several ways: by reducing the costs of present levels of productivity, by increasing the productivity for the same costs, or by increasing productivity at a proportionately greater rate for some increase in costs. A well established cost accounting system provides the costs for the existing system. The analyst need only determine the costs of the proposed system.

Proposed costs are normally divided into implementation or start-up costs, sometimes stated as "first-year costs," and operating costs. When proposed systems entail expenditures for major equipment, one of the elements of the cost study will be the cost of the equipment. This is normally distributed over the expected life of the equipment by amortizing the cost over five to ten years. The acquisition of a five thousand dollar tape activated typewriter, for example, is then included in the annual operating costs. If the ten year period is used, then five hundred dollars is included in the annual operating costs for equipment. Similarly, supplies that are extraordinary—other than the usual 3×5 slips, paper clips, and pencils—are also estimated for the year and included in the cost figure for the new system.

These kinds of costs are relatively fixed and usually present no difficulty beyond ferreting out the real costs from manufacturer's data. The more difficult aspects of projecting costs stem from the need to determine the time required by human operators of equipment, or the costs of performing manual tasks. This can be done by simulated time studies or by using such systems as Master Standard Data or Methods Time Measurement. Since the times are based on averages, it is advantageous to use relatively conservative estimates so that the actual performance exceeds the projections.

The sum of all the activity times together with the supplies and equipment costs represents the projected operating cost of the proposed system. These costs must be added to the implementation costs which vary for different types of systems. A new manual procedure will entail few problems in the implementation stage. A new data-processing system, however, requires estimates of programming time for in-house programming, program costs for packaged programs, debugging time, operator training, and equipment delivery schedules.

The implementation phase of the systems study can be a harrowing experience. It is the phase in which planning pays great dividends, for three laws are usually operative: everything takes longer than you expect, expect the unexpected and whatever can go wrong will. Whenever possible, it is desirable to run the proposed system in parallel with the existing system. This provides an opportunity to debug the system, verify the original cost estimates, and make adjustments in the system under operating conditions. Occasionally, there are compelling reasons for bypassing the parallel operation. One alternative is to divide the system into segments or modules and get one operating before proceeding to the next.

Cost data is a critical element in sound management. It should be an integral element of every new system installed in the library so that control systems become available for evaluating the systems in operation. It is doubly important that sound data be accumulated for proposed systems, for this represents one of the most effective means of justifying a change in operating systems. Since the decision to proceed with a new system entails a commitment to costs for the indefinite future, it is essential that the most accurate assessment of these costs be made so that the decision to implement is made with the greatest degree of certainty.

Selected Readings

Brutcher, Constance, et al. 1964. Cost accounting for the library. *Library resources and technical services* 8:413–31.

Burgess, Thomas K. 1973. A cost effectiveness model for comparing circulation studies. *Journal of library automation* 6:75–86.

Burkhalter, Barton R. 1968. Memo on effective labor costs. In *Case studies in systems analysis in a university library,* pp. 9–10. Metuchen, N. J.: Scarecrow.

Dougherty, R. M., ed. 1969. Cost analysis studies in libraries: Is there a basis for comparison? *Library resources and technical services* 13:136–41.

Dougherty, Richard M., and Heinritz, Fred J., 1966. Cost. In *Scientific management of library operations,* pp. 150–67. New York: Scarecrow.

Hayes, Robert M., and Becker, Joseph. 1974. Administrative data processing. In *Handbook of data processing for libraries,* pp. 383–414. 2d ed. Los Angeles: Melville.

Klintoe, Kjeld. 1971. Cost analysis of a technical information unit. *ASLIB proceedings* 23:362–71.

Kountz, John C. 1972. Library cost analysis: a recipe. *Library journal* 97:459–64.

Lock, William. 1970. Computer costs for large libraries. *Datamation* 16:69–74.

Mason, Ellsworth. 1971. The great gas bubble prick't or computers revealed, a gentleman of quality. *College and research libraries* 33:183–96.

Wilson, John H., Jr. 1972. Costs budgeting, and economics of information processing. In *Annual review of information science and technology,* vol. 7, pp. 39–67. Washington, D.C.

10. Evaluation

In the preceeding chapters, the theoretical assumptions on which the systems approach rests have been identified, as have the tools which can be used in studying the library. Then, the cost of performing the work required to transform inputs into outputs was examined. Our final consideration must be: Does it work? The answer is a qualified yes. It works because research is accomplished, new systems are designed, and new knowledge is discovered. The answer is qualified because we still do not know how well it works, whether or not another system might work better, or whether there is a simple, undiscovered element which might change the entire process. In our final chapter then, we examine the things we can and cannot evaluate. These divide roughly into the tangible or quantitative elements of the system and the intangible or qualitative elements of the system.

The quantitative measures are easy. A discrete count of products or service events can be obtained and the current volume of activity can be compared with the activity in prior periods. Such comparison indicates whether or not the system is being maintained at expected levels of production.

Furthermore, we can measure all of the elements of the input: work hours, supplies, equipment costs, rent and other tangible items which are translated into costs. These can be compared in relation to different methods or systems. The costs give half of the picture; it should also be determined, to the best of our ability, that the resources being used give the best benefit possible.

The best method for measuring the value or quality of the services a library provides is to ask the user. This has characteristically been most effective in the special library where a relatively restricted clientele can be surveyed, interviewed, or asked to maintain a diary of information needs. Within these special information service systems, it becomes possible to assess the effectiveness of the system in relation to the clientele's needs.

When an attempt to assess the more general large academic or public library is made, it is more difficult. The measures of effectiveness that will give an accurate evaluation of the services produced have not yet been determined. One of the difficulties is the subjective view of services that many users have. It is clear that a research person who has completed a book, for example, has obtained the references needed, compiled the bibliography of sources relevant to the task, and generally performed all of the functions associated with the completed book. It is not difficult to imagine, however, that two different researchers who have completed similar projects will have totally different perceptions of the library services they received. One may have demanded materials in esoteric journals, obtainable only from one or two other locations, and he may have presented his requests in garbled form which required repeated inquiries as to his intent. When the project is completed, he may assess the service as either poor or impossible, completely disregarding that much of the intermittent failure was caused by his own carelessness.

Another researcher may have presented inquiries for an equal number of interlibrary loans, but with accurate information or for publications that are more accessible. He may do all of these things with respect for the complexities of the bibliographic systems. The first researcher is negative in his reaction to the services received while the second is positive in his reaction to the services. It is not exactly the same service; the staff will respond to the second person differently from the way they react to the first. Whose assessment of the service will be accepted?

As we shall see, both are helpful. It is important to examine the negative reports of service; the user may be correct in his assessment. When the situation has been thoroughly examined, ways to improve methods may be found. Positive reports, however, need to be accepted with care; examination may disclose that the report commending the service is based on results that could still be improved. The system is in some way functional, but there is room for further refinement and improvement. This is a characteristic of systems work. When the new system is working smoothly, the systems analyst does not become lulled into a state of complacency. The new system becomes input, and the cycle begins again.

Each time a system is analysed, the ideal established in goals and objectives comes closer to realization. With each repetition of the cycle, new methods are explored. As a new system is designed and installed, new and better ways of evaluating the quality of the system output are sought.

What role does evaluation play
in systems analysis and design?

King and Bryant point out that:

> Systems components refer to specific items such as hardware, books, staff, and buildings. Each component may itself be the object of evaluation, or at least an important element in evaluation decisions. Evaluation processes may be used to compare two methods of implementing a particular component (e.g. two photocomposition devices). We cannot evaluate systems processes without also evaluating system components, since the processes are dependent upon the individual components. (84:4)

The evaluation of systems is incorporated into the elements

of the design. Regardless of the perspective of the analyst, e.g., management, engineering, information science, etc., the last step in the development of the system is the evaluation of its performance. If a model has been used, as in operations research and management science approaches, the evaluation may also be used to verify the accuracy of the model or to improve the model. Regardless of the methodology and techniques used, the system is evaluated and modified until its performance achieves the intended standards.

Performance reports may be incorporated into the system so that a continuing record becomes available. This data serves as the input for the monitoring systems for control purposes. After the system has settled into an operating mode, the regular production and performance reports show variations from one month, quarter, or year to the next. These serve as warning signals when the system does not perform well and steps need to be taken to return the system to normal condition. It is this idea of continuous control that we consider next.

How is evaluation related to library and information systems operations?

A continuing need in libraries is the development of objective criteria of evaluation which indicate the performance of the library in relation to the goals it is working to achieve. The evaluation process, whether on an *ad hoc* study basis or as an integral part of operations, provides the data on which sound decisions can be made. Furthermore, the availability of a systematic means of measuring performance permits experimentation which can then be evaluated objectively rather that subjectively. The need for objective measures is clear; without objective measures, arguments may be strongly influenced by subjective beliefs and notions of what ought to be. Resources are limited; the reality of the environment in which the library functions must be assessed. A large element of the environment is the public served by the library. Unless effective ways to accurately measure the services provided in terms that the public can comprehend are found the necessary resources cannot be justified.

*How can libraries use evaluation to aid
in the continuing improvement of services?*

Evaluation helps the library to improve its services by
providing objective measures of the effectiveness of methods
and services. It becomes necessary to examine all of the
possible ways in which library and information services can
be delivered to the client community. These methods of delivering services must then be evaluated to determine whether
or not they perform as the preinstallation analyses predicted
they would perform. The results of the post installation evaluation will show the degree to which the service or method
contributes to the goals and objectives of the library. At this
point, the library is able to determine the effectiveness of the
service or the efficiency of the methods designed to deliver
services. Evaluation will aid in the improvement of services
when an objective measure of services has been devised and
reaction to the results of measurement by modifying the
methods for greater efficiency, changing the services, stop-
ping ineffective operations, etc. takes place.

*What can the librarian do
to facilitate the evaluation process?*

The librarian is an integral part of the service organization
which offers library and information services. It is extremely
difficult to maintain sensitivity to the real needs of one's
clientele. Many individuals do not wish to understand the
internal processes of information services; they judge the
service on the results they get in response to their inquiry. The
librarian must be conscientious in providing the right information in the right form. At the same time, the librarian must
be sensitive to the way the organization functions, considering all of the methods used and continuously examining the
methods to make sure that the best means of delivering
information services are being used. One of the ways that the
librarian can facilitate the evaluation process is by keeping
accurate records of successes and failures so that the system
can be modified to reduce the failures which fit within the
intent of the library's objectives while increasing the successes of the library transactions with its client population.

Selected Readings

Chapman, Edward A., St. Pierre, Paul L., and Lubans, John, Jr. 1970. Evaluation of the current operating system and report of findings. In *Library systems analysis guidelines,* pp. 97-111. New York: Wiley.

Cooper, Michael D. 1972. A cost model for evaluating information retrieval systems. *Journal of the American society for information science* 23:306-12.

Gilchrist, A. 1971. Cost effectiveness. *ASLIB proceedings* 23:455-64.

Hayes, Robert M. and Becker, Joseph. 1974. System budgeting and evaluation. In *Handbook of data processing for libraries,* pp. 178-94. 2d ed. Los Angeles: Melville.

Myers, Rose. 1972. Library self evaluation. In *Quantitative methods in librarianship,* ed. Irene Braden and Alice S. Clark, pp. 61-65. New York: Greenwood Press.

Orr, Richard H., et al. 1968. Development of methodologic tools for planning and managing library services: I. Project goals and approach; II. Measuring a library's Capability for providing documents. *Bulletin of the medical libraries association* 56:241-67.

Reisman, A., et al. 1972. Timeliness of library materials delivery, a set of priorities. *Socio-economic planning sciences* 6:145-52.

Rosenberg, K. C. 1969. Evaluation of an industrial library, a simple minded technique. *Special libraries* 60:635-38.

Rzasa, Philip V., and Baker, Norman R. 1972. Measures of effectiveness for a university library. *Journal of the American society for information science* 23:248-53.

Salton, Gerard. 1975. System testing. In *Dynamic information and library processing,* pp. 215-33. Englewood Cliffs, N.J.: Prentice-Hall.

Salverson, Carol A. 1969. The relevance of statistics to library evaluation. *College and research libraries* 30:352-62.

Stevenson, C. C. 1967. Checklist for review and evaluation of technical libraries. *Special libraries* 58:106-10.

Urquhart, John A., and Schofield, J. L. 1971. Measuring reader's failure at the shelf. *Journal of documentation* 7:273-86.

Wessel, C. J. 1968. Criteria for evaluating technical library effectiveness. *ASLIB proceedings* 20:455-81.

Exercises

Systems Exercise No. 1

A cataloging system

The cataloging problem presented here is defined as the process from the receipt of the material in the cataloging department to the completion of the final cataloging copy. The book at this point is forwarded to a processing unit to prepare it for the shelves and the cataloging copy is forwarded to a production unit to reproduce cards for a divided catalog. It is assumed that the supplies, equipment, and space are available and do not represent a part of the problem. The analyst's task is to analyze the present system and to consider the possible ways in which the system can be modified to catalog a seventy-five percent increase in cataloging volume. The production statistics for the previous ten years are available to the analyst and presented in table 1. The present system is described in the following section.

The present system

Titles are received from acquisition with an indication of the results of the preorder search. Location of the title in NUC or any other publication providing full cataloging information is noted on the purchase order copy forwarded to cataloging with the book. The LC cataloging titles are routed to the paraprofessional staff who locate the cataloging copy, accept the copy as found, and prepare master copy for the typing staff. The titles for which no LC copy has been found by acquisitions are routed to the librarians. These are sorted into those which may have been cataloged subsequent to the acquisitions search and those for which LC cataloging will probably not be found. The first group are routed to the paraprofessional staff for searching. The second group are cataloged by the catalogers. If the paraprofessional does not find cataloging copy, the title is routed back to the cataloger. These two groups—those the librarian expected to find LC copy for and did not locate copy and those for which LC copy was not expected—become the "original cataloging." The remaining titles are "LC cataloging." Occasionally, a librarian finds copy when it is not expected and turns the work over to the paraprofessional to complete the cataloging.

The library

The college library has experienced steady growth in acquisitions during the last ten years. While backlogs have accumulated, they have not been serious although during some years the backlog has caused a problem. The standard work week is thirty-five hours per week and all staff receive four weeks vacation. The student population has shown a modest but steady increase as has the overall operating budget. This has been reflected in support for the library. While the needs of the cataloging department have not always been anticipated, they have been met when the evidence showed serious backlogs developing. The statistics show that staff was added more or less regularly from 1967 through 1977. The composition of the staff changed during this time and most of the added staff are paraprofessionals. In 1977, unanticipated events led to an increase in enrollment, and an expected seventy-five percent increase in cataloging volume. It would be possible to increase staff using the same basic pattern of staffing to meet this volume. The president and controller have indicated that this will not be feasible. Some funds are available, but not sufficient funds to increase the staff seventy-five percent. In order to find alternatives, the college has authorized the librarian to retain a systems analyst to study the situation and to make recommendations for a proposed system.

The problem

The problem of the systems analyst is to study the existing procedures for cataloging the new monographs (separates, continuations, etc.), investigate the costs for cataloging new titles and find alternative methods for cataloging. These are to be compared and a cataloging system designed which will meet the projected volume of thirty-five thousand titles per year. The goal of the study is to achieve the productive capacity for the projected volume at some cost less than that of a simple increase in staff. Supplies, space and other items are available and do not need to be included in the study. It is only necessary to determine the actual cataloging system and the ways in which it can be improved.

Table 1
CATALOGING STATISTICS, 1967–77

Year	Items	LC Cat.	Backlog	Orig. Cat.	Backlog	Lib. Asst.	Lns
1967	12892	7735	175	5156	175	1.5	2.5
1968	13536	8393	833	5143	163	1.5	2.5
1969	14213	9097	1537	5116	136	1.5	2.5
1970	14924	9850	230	5074	94	2.0	2.5
1971	15670	10656	576	5014	34	2.0	2.5
1972	16453	11518		4935		2.5	2.5
1973	17276	12439		4837		2.5	2.5
1974	18140	13424	824	4716		2.5	2.5
1975	19047	14476	1876*	4571		2.5	2.5
1976	20000	15600	480*	4400		3.0	2.5
1977	35000†	28000†		7000†	2020†	3.0	2.5

* Librarian reassigned to "LC cataloging" part time.
† Projected figures.

The presentation

When the study is completed, prepare a presentation for the library director, the president, and the controller, who will make the final decision. Include in the report a narrative text describing the present and the proposed systems and supplement the text with any appropriate system flow charts—graphic or tables, etc.—which explain the proposed system. Remember the president and controller are reasonably knowledgeable but do not understand or know all the details involved.

Systems Exercise No. 2

A new campus

A state university system, following the provisions of a master plan for higher education, has established a new campus. One of the early appointments made for the campus was the director of libraries. He had a year in which to plan the basic needs for the campus. Beginning in September of the current academic year, the acquisitions librarian began developing acquisitions systems which will be initiated in January. You have been appointed catalog librarian. You are responsible for designing the cataloging systems for the new campus. Your first task is to develop the staffing and organization for the department. This staff will be appointed to begin in the new fiscal year starting 1 July. Your second task will be to develop the methods and procedures for cataloging monographs. These will be implemented when the new staff begin in July. The target date for opening the campus to students is September of the next academic year.

Financial support is allocated for developing the monograph collection. The expected acquisiton rate is thirty-five thousand titles for the first three years, after which the normal acquisition rate will be contingent on the student enrollment. At the present time, the projected growth rate is eight percent per year for the next five years, after which it will begin to decline to a five percent growth rate during the succeeding five years.

You have been asked by the director to prepare a report showing the organization, staffing, and systems you will need to implement the program. While you may need to make projections about possible system developments, the plan is to be based on existing methods, sources, and technology. In addition to the narrative text describing the system you propose, the report should include adequate graphic presentations to provide for evaluation by the administration and the board of trustees.

Systems Exercise No. 3

Flowcharting

As a first step in developing the cataloging system for a university, the head of the cataloging department has tentatively divided the operations into four stages. These four stages have been subdivided into a series of actions. The stages and actions are listed below:

1. Precataloging activities
    1.1 Sort books
    1.2 Arrange books by subject
    1.3 Search for entries
    1.4 Forward books to cataloging
2. Cataloging activities
    2.1 Separate books into: *Rapid cataloging* (catalog card copy found in search)
    Original cataloging (no catalog card copy found in search)
    2.2 Original cataloging: Catalog items
    Prepare manuscript catalog card copy

> > Verify entry and subject terms in authority files.

2.3 Rapid cataloging: Catalog items
Locate catalog card copy in NUC, microfiche, MARC records, etc.
Verify entries and subject terms in authority file.

2.4 Revise catalog copy

3. Processing activities
3.1 Key punch circulation record (book card)
3.2 Verify book number in shelf list
3.3 Prepare item for loan
3.4 Forward to post cataloging
3.5 Forward book to circulation for shelving

4. Postcataloging activities
4.1 Type catalog card master from manuscript card
4.2 Reproduce catalog cards
4.3 Type headings on cards
4.4 Revise completed card sets
4.5 Add to statistics
4.6 File cards

In order to plan in more detail, it will be useful to have a flowchart of the operations in the cataloging department. Prepare the flowchart using the standard symbols and indicating the operations and decisions that will be needed as material moves through the department.

Systems Exercise No. 4

Work sampling

The director of your university library wants to know how much it costs to catalog a book when it is cataloged locally. Original (i.e., local) cataloging requires that the cataloger perform all the steps from establishing the entry, recording the entry in the proper form, etc. He has become excited about the possibilities of work sampling as a way of gathering data that can be used for his budget presentation. As a result of this enthusiasm, he has talked to the catalogers and the head of cataloging and has collected the data for a work sampling study. However, since ALA is meeting in Hawaii this year, he has found it extremely important that he attend the conference. He has left the forms on which the data was recorded with the following instructions.

The five forms that are attached have been used to make random observations of the catalogers doing original cataloging. You will note that the observation times are listed on the left of the form. Under each activity (category), there is a peg count or tally showing how many times that activity was observed on each day. It isn't important to know what each cataloger is doing; we only need to know how his time is being used. To complete the study, we need to compute the percentages for each activity for each day. Then we need to compute the cumulative percentages for each activity.

When we have the completed totals and the daily and cumulative percentages, we can determine the amount of time that the catalogers spend on each activity. Using their time as the total available hours for original cataloging, the percentage of the times each activity is observed is the percentage of time used for that activity. I would like you to do the following computations and prepare the control chart for subject cataloging (examine, classify, etc.) using table 2 preceeding the data sheets.

1. Compute the total number of observations for each activity for each day.
2. Compute the percentage of observations for each activity for each day.
3. Compute the cumulative total number of observations for each activity for each successive day.
4. Compute the percentage of the cumulative total number of observations for each activity for each successive day.

When you have completed these computations, use the percentage of the cumulative total number of observations for subject cataloging to prepare a control chart for this activity. Plot the daily percentages on the chart to determine whether or not the sample falls within the acceptable range.

The catalogers work an eight hour day. Can you determine how many minutes it takes for each title (i.e., to examine and classify it) if the production statistics show an average of thirty-four titles a day?

Determine the control limits for an activity using table 2 (seventy-five observations) and the percentage you compute. The control is the range between the quantity shown in the column added to and subtracted from the cumulative percentage for an activity. For example, an activity with a cumulative percentage of .30 shows 15.9 as the range in the column under 75. .159 added to .30 gives the upper limit; .159 subtracted from .30 gives the lower limit.

Table 2

Percentage of Total Time Occupied by Activity	Average Number of Daily Observations										
	65	70	75	80	85	90	95	100	110	120	130
1/99	3.7	3.6	3.4	3.3	3.2	3.1	3.1	3.0	2.8	2.7	2.6
2/98	5.2	5.0	4.8	4.7	4.6	4.4	4.3	4.2	4.0	3.8	3.7
3/97	6.3	6.1	5.9	5.7	5.6	5.4	5.3	5.1	4.9	4.7	4.5
4/96	7.3	7.0	6.8	6.6	6.4	6.2	6.0	5.9	5.6	5.4	5.2
5/95	8.1	7.8	7.5	7.3	7.1	6.9	6.7	6.5	6.2	6.0	5.7
6/94	8.8	8.5	8.2	8.0	7.7	7.5	7.3	7.1	6.8	6.5	6.2
7/93	9.5	9.1	8.8	8.6	8.3	8.1	7.9	7.7	7.3	7.0	6.7
8/92	10.1	9.7	9.4	9.1	8.8	8.6	8.4	8.1	7.8	7.4	7.1
9/91	10.6	10.3	9.9	9.6	9.3	9.0	8.8	8.5	8.2	7.8	7.5
10/90	11.2	10.8	10.4	10.1	9.8	9.5	9.2	8.9	9.6	8.2	7.9
11/89	11.6	11.2	10.8	10.5	10.2	9.9	9.6	9.3	8.9	8.6	8.2
12/88	12.1	11.7	11.3	10.9	10.6	10.3	10.0	9.7	9.3	8.9	8.6
13/87	12.5	12.1	11.6	11.3	10.9	10.6	10.4	10.1	9.6	9.2	8.8
14/86	12.9	12.4	12.0	11.6	11.3	11.0	10.7	10.4	9.9	9.5	9.1
15/85	13.3	12.8	12.4	12.0	11.6	11.3	11.0	10.7	10.2	9.8	9.4
16/84	13.6	13.1	12.7	12.3	11.9	11.6	11.3	11.0	10.5	10.0	9.6
17/83	14.0	13.5	13.0	12.6	12.2	11.9	11.5	11.3	10.7	10.3	9.9
18/82	14.3	13.8	13.3	12.9	12.5	12.1	11.8	11.5	11.0	10.5	10.1
19/81	14.6	14.1	13.6	13.2	12.8	12.4	12.1	11.8	11.2	10.7	10.3
20/80	14.9	14.5	13.9	13.5	13.1	12.5	12.3	11.9	11.4	11.0	10.5
21/79	15.2	14.6	14.1	13.7	13.3	12.9	12.5	12.2	11.7	11.2	10.7
22/78	15.4	14.8	14.3	13.9	13.5	13.1	12.8	12.4	11.8	11.3	10.9
23/77	15.7	15.1	14.6	14.1	13.7	13.3	13.0	12.6	12.0	11.5	11.1
24/76	15.9	15.3	14.8	14.3	13.9	13.5	13.1	12.8	12.2	11.7	11.2
25/75	16.1	15.5	15.0	14.5	14.1	13.7	13.3	13.0	12.4	11.9	11.4
26/74	16.3	15.7	15.2	14.7	14.3	13.9	13.5	13.2	12.5	12.0	11.5
27/73	16.5	15.9	15.4	14.9	14.4	14.0	13.7	13.3	12.7	12.2	11.7
28/72	16.7	16.1	15.6	15.1	14.6	14.2	13.8	13.5	12.8	12.3	11.8
29/71	16.9	16.3	15.7	15.2	14.8	14.3	14.0	13.6	13.0	12.4	11.9
30/70	17.1	16.4	15.9	15.4	14.9	14.5	14.1	13.7	13.1	12.5	12.1
31/69	17.2	16.6	16.0	15.5	15.0	14.6	14.2	13.9	13.2	12.7	12.2
32/68	17.4	16.7	16.2	15.6	15.2	14.8	14.4	14.0	13.3	12.8	12.3
33/67	17.5	16.9	16.3	15.8	15.3	14.9	14.5	14.1	13.4	12.9	12.4
34/66	17.6	17.0	16.4	15.9	15.4	15.0	14.6	14.2	13.5	13.0	12.5
35/65	17.7	17.1	16.5	16.0	15.5	15.1	14.7	14.3	13.6	13.1	12.5
36/64	17.9	17.2	16.6	16.1	15.6	15.2	14.8	14.4	13.7	13.1	12.6
37/63	18.0	17.3	16.7	16.2	15.7	15.3	14.9	14.5	13.8	13.2	12.7
38/62	18.1	17.4	16.8	16.3	15.8	15.3	14.9	14.6	13.9	13.3	12.8
39/61	18.1	17.5	16.9	16.4	15.9	15.4	15.0	14.6	14.0	13.4	12.8
40/60	18.2	17.6	17.0	16.4	15.9	15.5	15.1	14.7	14.0	13.4	12.9
41/59	18.3	17.6	17.0	16.5	16.0	15.6	15.1	14.8	14.1	13.5	12.9
42/58	18.4	17.7	17.1	16.6	16.1	15.6	15.2	14.8	14.1	13.5	13.0
43/57	18.4	17.8	17.1	16.6	16.1	15.7	15.2	14.9	14.2	13.6	13.0
44/56	18.5	17.8	17.2	16.6	16.2	15.7	15.3	14.9	14.2	13.6	13.1
45/55	18.5	17.8	17.2	16.7	16.2	15.7	15.3	14.9	14.2	13.6	13.1
46/54	18.5	17.9	17.3	16.7	16.2	15.8	15.3	15.0	14.3	13.6	13.1
47/53	18.6	17.9	17.3	16.7	16.2	15.8	15.4	15.0	14.3	13.7	13.1
48/52	18.6	17.9	17.3	16.8	16.3	15.8	15.4	15.0	14.3	13.7	13.1
49/51	18.6	17.9	17.3	16.8	16.3	15.8	15.4	15.0	14.3	13.7	13.2
50/50	18.6	17.9	17.3	16.8	16.3	15.8	15.4	15.0	14.3	13.7	13.2

Work Sampling Data Sheet

	Department __Cataloging__		Date __3/28/77__		Day __1__			
	Number of Persons __3__		Remarks _____					

Times	Category	Tally	Total	%	Totals prior	today	Cum. %
8:20 8:50 9:20	Search	~~HH~~ IIII					
9:45 9:55 10:00	Copy	III					
10:30 10:40 11:10	Describe	~~HH~~ ~~HH~~ II					
11:30 11:40 11:50	Examine, Classify	~~HH~~ ~~HH~~ I					
1:05 1:15 1:20	Locate #	II					
1:25 1:30 1:35	Select s. h.	~~HH~~ I					
2:20 2:35 3:15	Record	III					
3:40 3:45 4:10	Write Card copy	~~HH~~ IIII					
4:35	Other	~~HH~~ ~~HH~~					
	Grand totals						
	Notes						

Search: Search authority files and reference sources for correct form of entry.
Copy: Record the correct form of entry.
Describe: Record the bibliographic description of the work.
Examine, Classify: Examine the work and select the appropriate classification number for it.
Locate: Find the correct number from classification schedules.
Select s.h.: Select the proper subject headings from subject heading list.
Record: Record classification number and subject headings.
Write card copy: Write out the bibliographic description, classification, and tracing in final form for card production.
Other: Talking, waiting, personal time, rest periods, etc.

Work Sampling Data Sheet

	Department Cataloging		Date 3/29/77		Day 2		

Number of Persons ___3___   Remarks _____

Times	Category	Tally	Total	%	Totals prior	today	Cum. %
8:05 8:20	Search	HHt HHt ll					
8:55 9:10 9:20	Copy	l					
9:35 10:30 11:05	Describe	HHt HHt					
11:15 11:25 11:45	Examine, Classify	HHt HHt HHt l					
1:00 1:10 1:35	Locate #	lll					
1:55 2:00 2:05 2:35	Select s. h.	HHt llll					
2:55 3:20	Record	lll					
3:45 3:50 4:10	Write Card copy	HHt ll					
4:25	Other	HHt HHt ll					
	Grand totals						
	Notes						

Search: Search authority files and reference sources for correct form of entry.
Copy: Record the correct form of entry.
Describe: Record the bibliographic description of the work.
Examine, Classify: Examine the work and select the appropriate classification number for it.
Locate: Find the correct number from classification schedules.
Select s.h.: Select the proper subject headings from subject heading list.
Record: Record classification number and subject headings.
Write card copy: Write out the bibliographic description, classification, and tracing in final form for card production.
Other: Talking, waiting, personal time, rest periods, etc.

Work Sampling Data Sheet

	Department __Cataloging__	Date __3/30/77__	Day __3__					
	Number of Persons __3__		Remarks _____					

Times	Category	Tally	Total	%	Totals prior	Totals today	Cum. %
8:10 8:35	Search	⨿⨿ ⨿⨿ I					
8:55 9:00 9:10	Copy	I					
9:45 10:00 10:05	Describe	⨿⨿ ⨿⨿ I					
10:50 11:00 11:20	Examine, Classify	⨿⨿ ⨿⨿ I					
11:30 1:40 1:45	Locate #	III					
1:55 2:00 2:55 3:00	Select s. h.	⨿⨿ ⨿⨿ I					
3:05 3:35	Record	II					
3:40 4:10 4:35 4:50	Write Card copy	III					
	Other	⨿⨿ IIII					
	Grand totals						
	Notes						

Search: Search authority files and reference sources for correct form of entry.
Copy: Record the correct form of entry.
Describe: Record the bibliographic description of the work.
Examine, Classify: Examine the work and select the appropriate classification number for it.
Locate: Find the correct number from classification schedules.
Select s.h.: Select the proper subject headings from subject heading list.
Record: Record classification number and subject headings.
Write card copy: Write out the bibliographic description, classification, and tracing in final form for card production.
Other: Talking, waiting, personal time, rest periods, etc.

Work Sampling Data Sheet

	Department Cataloging		Date 3/31/77			Day 4		
	Number of Persons 3		Remarks					
Times	Category	Tally	Total	%	Totals prior	Totals today	Cum. %
8:15 8:25	Search	̶H̶H̶ ̶H̶H̶ II					
9:20 9:40 9:55	Copy	III					
10:00 10:30 10:50	Describe	̶H̶H̶ IIII					
11:10 11:45 11:50	Examine, Classify	̶H̶H̶ ̶H̶H̶ ̶H̶H̶ ̶H̶H̶ ̶H̶H̶ II					
1:30 1:40 2:10	Locate #	̶H̶H̶					
2:20 2:30 2:45 2:50	Select s. h.	̶H̶H̶ I					
3:15 3:20	Record	I					
3:25 3:50 4:30	Write Card copy	̶H̶H̶ ̶H̶H̶ IIII					
4:45 4:55	Other	̶H̶H̶ ̶H̶H̶ I					
	Grand totals						
	Notes						

Search: Search authority files and reference sources for correct form of entry.
Copy: Record the correct form of entry.
Describe: Record the bibliographic description of the work.
Examine, Classify: Examine the work and select the appropriate classification number for it.
Locate: Find the correct number from classification schedules.
Select s.h.: Select the proper subject headings from subject heading list.
Record: Record classification number and subject headings.
Write card copy: Write out the bibliographic description, classification, and tracing in final form for card production.
Other: Talking, waiting, personal time, rest periods, etc.

Work Sampling Data Sheet

	Department Cataloging		Date 4/1/77			Day 5		
	Number of Persons 3		Remarks					

Times	Category	Tally	Total	%	Totals prior	today	Cum. %
8:05 8:25	Search	‖‖ ‖‖					
8:45 9:05 9:50	Copy	‖‖ ‖					
10:10 10:20 10:30	Describe	‖‖ ‖‖ ‖‖					
10:35 10:50 11:00	Examine, Classify	‖‖ ‖‖ ‖‖ ‖‖ ‖					
11:10 11:40 11:45	Locate #	‖					
1:00 1:45 1:50 2:00	Select s. h.	‖‖ ‖‖ ‖					
2:35 2:45 3:00	Record	‖‖ ‖					
3:45 3:55 4:30	Write Card copy	‖‖ ‖‖ ‖					
4:35	Other	‖‖ ‖‖					
	Grand totals						
	Notes						

Search: Search authority files and reference sources for correct form of entry.
Copy: Record the correct form of entry.
Describe: Record the bibliographic description of the work.
Examine, Classify: Examine the work and select the appropriate classification number for it.
Locate: Find the correct number from classification schedules.
Select s.h.: Select the proper subject headings from subject heading list.
Record: Record classification number and subject headings.
Write card copy: Write out the bibliographic description, classification, and tracing in final form for card production.
Other: Talking, waiting, personal time, rest periods, etc.

Systems Exercise No. 5

PERT

One of the techniques used for scheduling projects is PERT. The system—Program Evaluation Review Technique—uses network charts and time estimates to show the time required to complete a total project. PERT is also used as an operational monitoring system. In this exercise, it is treated as a part of operations. There are three levels to the exercise: (1) break down the events used in the Gantt chart into an events list, (2) arrange the events in a logical sequence showing parallel and sequential operations (parallel operations are those which can be carried on at the same time; sequential operations are those in which one step must be completed before the next step can begin), (3) connect the events in a network chart showing the activities that are required to complete the process.

A complete PERT program also requires that the time for each activity be estimated at three levels: optimistic (best time), pessimistic (worst time), and most likely time. With the complete PERT network chart, it becomes possible to develop critical paths to show those activities which effectively control the progress on a project. In this operational version of PERT, you are to develop a chart which shows: (1) the events, (2) the logical sequence of events with the appropriate bursting of processing flow and the merging of activities into a single event, and (3) the activities connecting the events. Develop the chart from the PERT Work Sheet.

Table 3

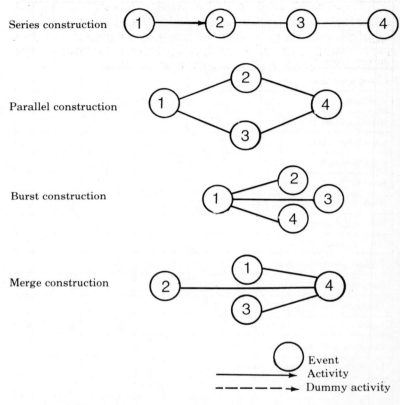

Series construction

Parallel construction

Burst construction

Merge construction

Event
Activity
Dummy activity

t_o (O.T.)=Optimistic time: Time estimate when no unforeseen problems arise. Chances are 1 in 100.

t_m (M.L.T.)=Most Likely Time: Time under normal conditions.

t_p (P.T.)=Pessimistic Time: Time estimate in adverse conditions. Chances are 1 in 100

t_e (E.A.T.)=Expected Activity Time: $t_e = (t_o + 4t_m + t_p)/6$

T_E (E.E.T.) = Expected event time: $T_E = $ $T_E = T_{e1} + T_{e2} + T_{e3} \ldots T_{en}$

T_L (L.A.T.) = Latest allowable time: $T_L = T_S - T_E$

T_S (S.T.)=Scheduled time: T_S

S = Slack: $S = T_L - T_E$

ACTIVITIES

	t_o	t_m	t_p	t_e	T_L	T_E	S
Start							
Receive books							
Check proof sheet							
Sort books							
Arrange books by subject							
Search for entries							
Copy entries for LC books							
Send LC books to rapid							
Send "originals" to "OC"							
"OC" catalog—descriptive							
"OC" catalog—subject							
Prepare manuscript copy							
Proofread (and correct)							
Verify main entry in authority file							
Verify subjects in authority file							
Dispatch "OC" to end processing							
LC items—locate catalog entries							
Copy: NUC, MARC, etc.							
Verify main entry in authority file							
Verify subject in authority file							
Dispatch LC to end processing							
Keypunch books cards							
Verify book number in shelf list							
Type call # and accession # lables							
Type call # on book card jacket							
Paste call # label on spine							

ACTIVITIES

	t_o	t_m	t_p	t_e	T_L	T_E	S
Paste book jacket on verso of cover							
Paste date due sheet							
Spray lettered book							
Stamp							
Send books to be shelved							
Send manuscript card to post cat.							
Proofread manuscript card							
Type catalog card from manuscript							
Proofread master catalog card							
Reproduce cards (xerox)							
Type added entries on cards							
Type subject headings on cards							
Separate cards and proofread							
Count cards and add to statistics							
Sort cards alphabetically							
File in main card catalog							
File in shelf list							
Cards sent to other files							
Check filing errors							
Filing completed							
Stop							

Systems Exercise No. 6

Organization design

The director of a new academic library (four year liberal arts college with master's degree programs) has assigned responsibility to the head of cataloging for developing the staffing tables that will be needed to catalog and process new materials for the library. You, as head of cataloging, have gained experience with scheduling (Gantt charts, PERT, etc.) and work sampling in previous assignments. Now you are expected to develop the staffing for this new campus so that personnel can be recruited and selected. The library anticipates a processing and cataloging work load of thirty-five thousand titles.

Design the organization you will use and prepare an organization chart showing the lines of communication, the responsibility of each person, and the number and levels of staff that you will need. You will, of course, be responsible for recruiting and participating in the selection of the staff and will need position descriptions for each class of employee and for each supervisory position. The staffing you are proposing is based on a manual system for cataloging and processing.

Systems Exercise No. 7

Unit costs

Scanning the library literature, you discover a wide range of costs for cataloging and processing. Cataloging, for example, ranges from four dollars to twenty dollars per title. In addition, costs have risen very rapidly over the last decade. The director of your academic library wants you as head of cataloging to compute the unit costs for processing a title completely from cataloging to shelf-ready state. The president has asked for detailed costs from all of the department heads on this new campus so he can begin working on the next budget.

You will need to identify all the costs involved in this manual system for cataloging and processing to justify the staffing table you have proposed. You will remember that each position entails costs for insurance and other fringe benefits. The unit costs for the manual system also entails such items as the costs of cards, etc. Develop the unit cost showing the distribution of all of the personnel and supplies costs for cataloging and processing.

Systems Exercise No. 8

Alternative systems

The president of the university has come back to the library director after talking to the director of the computing center. The president has accepted the computer man's argument that the costs are too high for the manual cataloging system. He has asked the library director to investigate the possible cost savings by using the on-line system for cataloging. Using your previous studies, compare the costs you might be able to achieve by using OCLC, SPIRES-BALLOTS, MINI-MARC, or other similar sources of cataloging data.

The library director wants you to show the manual and the automated systems and to indicate what will be needed to implement the computer system you propose. Include both cataloging and processing in your plan.

Bibliography

1. Ackoff, Russell L. 1971. Towards a system of systems concepts. *Management science* 17:661-71.
2. ———, and Sasieni, Maurice W. 1968. *Fundamentals of operations research.* New York: Wiley.
3. Adelson, Marvin. 1968. The systems approach: a perspective. *Wilson library bulletin* 42:711-15.
4. Allen, A. H. 1972. Systems to manage the industrial library. *Journal of systems management* 23:24-27.
5. Allen, T. J., and Gerstberger, P. G. 1967. *Criteria for selection of an information source.* Cambridge, Mass.: M.I.T. Alfred P. Sloane School of Management.
6. Alper, Bruce H. 1975. Library automation. In *Annual review of information science and technology,* vol. 10. Washington, D.C.: American Society for Information Science.
7. American Library Association. 1965-. *Library technology reports.*
8. American Society for Information Science. 1971. *Key papers in information science.* Ed. Arthur W. Elias. Washington, D. C.

9. American Society for Information Science and National Federation of Abstracting and Indexing Services. 1973. *Key papers on the use of computer-based bibliographic services.* Ed. Stella Keenan. Washington, D. C.

10. Anderla, G. 1973. *Information in 1985: a forecasting study of information needs and resources.* Paris: Organization for Economic Cooperation and Development.

11. Andrews, T. 1968. The role of departmental libraries in operations research studies in a university library; Part I: Selection for storage problems; Part II: A statistical study of book use. *Special libraries* 59:519-24.

12. Applegate, H. C. *The cost-effectiveness of field pickup of long overdue items at the Glendale Public Library.* Glendale, Calif.: Glendale Public Library.

13. Arms, W. Y. 1975. Operational research in libraries. *Studies of library management,* vol. 2, pp. 76-91. Hamden, Conn.

14. Armstrong, Charles M. 1968. Measurement and evaluation of the public library. In *Research methods in librarianship: measurement and evaluation,* ed. Herbert Goldhor. Champaign, Ill.: University of Illinois Graduate School of Library Science.

15. Aro, Barbara, et al. 1965. *Cost analysis study.* Studies in Librarianship no. 4. Denver, Colo.: University of Denver Library.

16. Arora, S. R., and Paul, R. N. 1969. Acquisitions of library materials: a quantitative approach. In *ASIS proceedings* (San Francisco, 1969), pp. 495-99. Westport, C.T.: Greenwood Press.

17. Artandi, Susan. 1972. *An introduction to computers in information science.* 2nd ed. Metuchen, N.J.: Scarecrow.

18. ASLIB Research Department. 1970. The analysis of library processes. *Journal of documentation* 26:30-45.

19. Ayres, F. H. 1970. Some basic laws of library automation. *Program* 4:68-69.

20. Baaske, J. Tolliver, D. L., and Westerberg, J. 1974. Overdue policies: a comparison of alternatives. *College and research libraries.* 35:354-59
21. Baker, G. G. 1974. Information access methods for microfilm systems. *Microdoc* 13:100-12.
22. Baker, N. R. 1969. Optimal user search sequences and implications for information systems operation. *American documentation* 20:203-12.
23. Baumol, W. J., and Marcus, M. 1973. *Economics of academic libraries.* Washington, D. C.: American Council on Education.
24. Becker, Joseph. 1965. Systems analysis, prelude to library data processing. *ALA bulletin* 59:293-96.
25. ———, and Pulsifer, Josephine. 1974. *Application of computer technology to library processes.* Metuchen, N.J.: Scarecrow.
26. Beeler, M. G. Fancher, et al. 1974. *Measuring the quality of library services: a handbook.* Metuchen, N.J.: Scarecrow.
27. Bellomy, Fred L. 1969. Management planning for library system development. *Journal of library automation* 2:187-217.
28. ———. 1968. The systems approach to library operation. *ALA bulletin* 62:1121-25.
29. Benton, John D. 1973. *Managing the organizational decision process.* Toronto: Lexington Books.
30. Bergen, D. 1966. Implications of general systems theory for librarianship and higher education. *College and research libraries* 27:358-88.
31. Bernstein, H. H. 1971. Some organizational prerequisites for the introduction of electronic data processing in libraries. *Libri* 21:15-25.
32. Bertalanffy, Ludwig Von. 1968. *General systems theory: foundations, development, applications.* New York: George Braziller.
33. ———. 1968. The history and status of general systems theory. In *General systems theory: foundations, development, applications.* Also in: Cougar, J. Daniel and Knapp, Robert W., eds. 1974. *Systems Analysis*

Techniques. New York: Wiley; and Kliv, G. J., ed. 1972. *Trends in general systems theory.* New York: Wiley.

34. Bohl, Marilyn. 1971. *Flow-Charting techniques.* Chicago: Science Research Associates.
35. Bolles. S. W. 1967. The use of flow-charts in the analysis of library operations. *Special libraries* 58:95-98.
36. Bommer, M. R. W. 1972. *The development of a management system for effective decision making in a university library.* Ann Arbor, Mich.: University Microfilms.
37. Bookstein, Abraham. 1974. Allocation of resources in an information system. *ASIS journal* 25:52-58.
38. ———. 1973. Models for shelf reading. *Library quarterly* 43:126-37.
39. ———, and Swanson, D. R., 1973. A stochastic shelf reading model. *Library quarterly* 43:138-61.
40. Booth, A. D. 1969. On the geometry of libraries. *Journal of documentation* 25:28-42.
41. Bose, A. 1970. *An information system design methodology based on PERT/CPM networking and optimization techniques.* Doctoral Dissertation, University of Pittsburg.
42. Bourne, Charles P. 1970. *Data collection and cost modeling for library circulation systems.* Washington, D.C.: Office of Education, Bureau of Research, U. S. Department of Health, Education and Welfare.
43. ———. 1965. Some user requirements stated quantitatively in terms of the 90% library. In *Electronic information handling,* ed. A. Kent and O. Taulbee. Washington, D. C.: Spartan Books.
44. Braden, Irene, and Clark, Alice S. 197 . *Quantitative methods in librarianship.* New York: Greenwood Press.
45. Brett, V. M., et al. 1976. *The academic library: a systems view.* University of Lancaster Library Occasional Papers, no. 8. Lancaster, England: University Library.
46. Brittain, J. M. 1970. *Information and its users: a review*

with special reference to the social sciences. Bath: Bath University.

47. ————, and Line, M. B. 1973. Sources of citations and references for analysis purposes: a comparative assessment. *Journal of documentation* 29:72–80.

48. Brockis, G. J., and Cole, P. F. 1967. Evaluating the technical information function. *Chemistry in Britain* 3:421–23.

49. Bromberg, Erik. 1971. *Simplified PPBS for the librarian.* Prepared for Dollar Decision Pre-Conference Institute, sponsored by the Library Administration Division of the American Library Association, Dallas, Texas, 17–19 June 1971. Washington, D. C.: Educational Resources Information Science.

50. Brookes, B. C. 1969. Bradford's Law and the bibliography of science. *Nature* 224:953–55.

51. ————. 1969. The complete Bradford-Zipf "Bibliography." *Journal of documentation* 25:58–60.

52. ————. 1968. The derivation and application of the Bradford-Zipf distribution. *Journal of documentation* 24:247–65.

53. ————. 1970. The design of cost-effective hierarchial information systems. *Information and storage retrieval* 6:127–36.

54. Brophy, P., et al. eds. 1976. *Reader in operations research for libraries.* Washington, D. C.: NCR Microcard.

55. Brownlow, Jane L. 1960. Cost analysis for libraries. *DC libraries* 31:54–60.

56. Brush, William H. 1968. Work measurement. In *Systems and procedures: a handbook for business and industry,* ed. Victor Lazzaro, pp. 143–81. Englewood Cliffs: Prentice-Hall.

57. Brutcher, Constance, et al. 1964. Cost accounting for the library. *Library resources and technical services* 8:413–31.

58. Buckland, M. K. 1973. Are scattering and obsolescence related? *Journal of documentation* 29:107–109.

59. Buckland, M. K. 1975. *Book availability and the library user.* New York: Pergamon.

60. ———. 1973. Library systems and management studies at Lancaster University. In *A world of information: proceedings of the 35th annual meeting of the ASIS* (Washington, D.C., October 1972), pp. 131–34. Westport, Ct.: Greenwood Press.

61. ———. 1972. An operations research study of variable loan and duplication policy at the University of Lancaster. *Library quarterly* 42:97–106.

62. ———. 1975. Toward an economic theory of the library. In *Symposium on the economics of information dissemination* (Syracuse, 1973). Syracuse: Syracuse University Press.

63. ———, and Hindle, A. 1971. The case for library management games. *Journal of education for librarianship* 21:92–103.

64. ———, and Hindle, A. 1969. A library zipf. *Journal of documentation* 25:52–57.

65. ———, and Woodburn, I. 1968. *Some implications for library management of scattering and obsolescence.* University of Lancaster Library Occasional Papers, no. 1. Lancaster, England: University Library.

66. ———, et al. 1970. *Systems analysis of a university library.* University of Lancaster Library occasional papers, no. 4. Lancaster, England: University Library.

67. Bundy, M. L., and Wasserman, P. eds. 1970. *Reader in research methods for librarianship.* Washington, D. C.: NCR Microcard.

68. Burkhalter, B. K. 1968. *Case studies in systems analysis in a university library.* Metuchen, N. J.: Scarecrow.

69. Burgess, Thomas K. 1973. A cost effectiveness model for comparing various circulation studies. *Journal of library automation* 6:75–86.

70. Burns, Robert W., Jr. 1971. A generalized methodology for library systems analysis. *College and research libraries* 32:295–303.

71. Burr, Robert L. 1973. Librarians, libraries and librarianship: a model. *Libri* 23:181–209.

72. Bush, Vannevar. 1945. As we may think. *Atlantic monthly* 176: 101-108.
73. Busha, Charles, and Purcell, R. 1972. *The scientific investigation of library problems*. Bloomington, Ind.: Graduate Library School, University of Indiana.
74. California, University of Santa Barbara. 1971. *Library systems definition: functions and interfaces*. Santa Barbara, California.
75. Carlson, Robert D., and Lewis, James A. 1973. Definition of systems and project specifications. In *The systems analysis workbook: a complete guide to project implementation and control*, pp. 39-45. Englewood Cliffs, N.J.: Prentice-Hall.
76. Carroll, J. M. 1967. Methodology for information systems analysis. *Journal of industrial engineering* 18:650-57.
77. Carter, Ruth C. 1973. System analysis as a prelude to library automation. *Library trends* 21:505-21.
78. Castagna, Edwin. 1969. Nothing to lose but our routines: work simplification at the Long Beach Public Library. *ALA bulletin* 53:197-200.
79. Cavender, T. P. 1965. Time and motion techniques related to costs of expanding the card catalog. *Library resources and technical services* 1:104-108.
80. Chamis, A. Y. 1969. Design of information systems: the use of systems analysis. *Special libraries* 60:29-31.
81. Chapin, Ned. 1974. Flowcharting with the ANSI standard: a tutorial. In *Systems analysis techniques,* ed. J. D. Cougar and R. D. Knapp, pp. 129-61. New York: Wiley.
82. Chapman, Edward A. 1973. Planning for system development. *Library trends* 21:479-92.
83. ———, et al. 1969. *Systems analysis and design as related to library operations. LARC Report, no. 2.*
84. ———, St. Pierre, Paul, and Lubans, John, Jr. 1970. *Library systems analysis guidelines*. New York: Wiley.
85. Chen, Ching-chih. 1976. *Applications of operations research models to libraries: a case study of the use of*

monographs in the Francis A. Countway Library of Medicine, Harvard University. Cambridge, Mass.: M.I.T. Press.

86. Churchman, C. West. 1968. *The systems approach.* New York: Delacorte Press.

87. Clapp, V. W., and Jordon, R. T. 1965. Quantitative criteria for adequacy of academic library collections. *College and research libraries* 26:371-80.

88. Cleland, David I., and King, William R. 1968. *Systems analysis and project management.* New York: McGraw-Hill.

89. Clerverdon, Cyril W. 1974. User evaluation of information retrieval systems. *Journal of documentation* 30:170-80.

90. Clinton, M. 1972. Study of the effect of fines on circulation. *Canadian library journal* 29:248-52.

91. Cole, P. F. 1958. Analysis of reference question records as a guide to the information requirements of scientists. *Journal of documentation* 14:197-207.

92. Columbia University Libraries. 1964. *A description of a project to study the research library as an economic system.* New York: Columbia University Libraries.

93. Cooper, Michael D. 1972. A cost model for evaluating information retrieval systems. *ASIS journal* 23:306-12.

94. Corey, James F., and Bellomy, Fred L. 1973. Determining requirements for a new system. *Library trends* 21:533-52.

95. Cougar, J. Daniel. 1974. Evolution of business system analysis techniques. In *Systems analysis techniques,* ed. J. D. Cougar and R. W. Knapp, pp. 63-85. New York: Wiley.

96. Cougar, J. Daniel, and Knapp, Robert W. eds. 1974. *Systems analysis techniques.* New York: Wiley.

97. Covill, George W. 1967. Librarian + systems analyst = teamwork. *Special libraries* 58:99-101.

98. Cox, N. S. M., et al. 1967. *The computer and the library.* Newcastle upon Tyne; Hamden, Conn.: Archon Books.

99. Cuadra, Carlos A. 1971. On-line systems: promise and pitfalls. *ASIS Journal* 22:107-14.
100. Daiute, R. J., and Gorman, K. A. 1974. *Library operations research.* Dobbs Ferry, N.Y.: Oceana Publications.
101. Davis, Charles H. 1974. *Illustrative computer programming for libraries.* Westport, Conn.: Greenwood Press.
102. De Gennaro, Richard. 1968. The development and administration of automated systems in academic libraries. *Journal of Library automation* 1:75-91.
103. Demos, John T. 1972. A study of bindery operations. In *Quantitative methods in librarianship: standards, research, management,* ed. Irene B. Hoadley et al. Westport, Conn.: Greenwood Press.
104. Dillehay, B. H., et al. 1970. Determining tomorrow's needs through today's requests: an automated approach to interlibrary loans. *Special libraries* 61:238-43.
105. Dodd, K. N. 1969. *Computer programming and languages.* New York: Plenum Press.
106. Dougherty, Richard M. 1970. Is work simplification alive and well someplace? *American libraries* 2:969-71.
107. ———. 1968. Manpower utilization in technical services. *Library resources and technical services* 12:77-82.
108. ———, and Heinritz, Fred J. 1966. *Scientific Management of Library Operations.* New York: Scarecrow.
109. ———, and Blomquist, Laura L. 1974. *Improving access to library resources: the influence of organization of library collections, and of user attitude toward innovative services.* Metuchen, N.J.: Scarecrow.
110. Drott, M. Carl. 1969. Random sampling: a tool for library research. *College and research libraries* 30:119-25.
111. Duchesue, Roderick M. 1973. Analysis of costs and performance. *Library trends* 21:587-604.
112. Elman, S. A. 1975. Cost comparison of manual and on-

line computerized literature searching. *Special libraries* 66:12-18.

113. Elson, Mark. 1973. Introduction to programming languages. In *Concepts of programming languages,* pp. 1-63. Chicago: Science Research Associates.

114. Emery, F. E., ed. 1970. *Systems thinking.* Harmondsworth, Middlesex, England: Penguin Books.

115. Emery, J. 1974. Cost/Benefit analysis of information systems. In *Systems analysis techniques,* eds. J. D. Cougar and R. W. Knapp, pp. 395-425. New York: Wiley.

116. Erisman, Robert E. 1971. *Returning the circulated book to the shelf: a study of the shelving operation in a university library.* Denver: University of Denver, Graduate School of Librarianship.

117. Evans, E., Borko, H. and Ferguson, P. 1972. A review of the criteria used to measure library effectiveness. *Bulletin of the Medical Library Association* 60:102-10.

118. Everts, Harry F. 1967. *Introduction to PERT.* Boston, Mass.: Allyn and Bacon.

119. Farino, Mario V. 1970. *Flow-Charting.* Englewood Cliffs, N.J.: Prentice-Hall.

120. Farradane, Jason. 1974. The evaluation of information retrieval systems. *Journal of documentation* 30:195-209.

121. Fasana, Paul J. 1973. Systems analysis. *Library trends* 21:465-78.

122. Fergus, Raymond M. 1976. Decision tables—what, why and how. In *Systems analysis techniques,* ed. J. D. Cougar and R. W. Knapp, pp. 162-79. New York: Wiley.

123. Fitzgerald, John M., and Fitzgerald, Andra F. 1973. *Fundamentals of systems analysis.* New York: Wiley.

124. Flood, Merrill M. 1964. Systems approach to library planning. *Library quarterly* 34:326-38.

125. Ford, G. 1973. *Library automation: guidelines to costing.* England, British Library Lending Division.

126. Ford, M. F. 1973. Research in user behavior in university libraries. *Journal of documentation* 29:85-106.

127. Ford, M. G. 1969. Data collection and feedback. In *Planning library services: proceedings of a research seminar, Lancaster, 1969,* eds. A. G. Mackenzie and I. M. Stuart. University of Lancaster Library occasional papers, No. 3. Lancaster, England: University Library.

128. Foskett, D. J. 1974. General systems theory and the organization of libraries. In *Studies in library management,* vol. 2, pp. 10–24. London: Bingley, Hamden, Conn.: Linnet Books.

129. Fried. L. 1971. How to analyze computer project costs. *Computer decisions* 8:22–26.

130. George, F. H. 1968. *An introduction to computer programming.* London: Pergamon.

131. Gilchrist, Alan. 1971. Cost-Effectiveness. *ASLIB proceedings* 23:455–64.

132. Gimbel, Henning. 1969. *Work simplification in Danish public libraries.* Translated by Randolph C. Ellsworth. Chicago: ALA.

133. Goddard, Haynes C. 1971. An economic analysis of library benefits. *Library quarterly* 41:244–55.

134. Golden, Barbara. 1974. A method for quantitatively evaluating a university library collection. *Library resources and technical services* 18:268–74.

135. Goffman, W., and Morris, T. G. 1970. Bradford's Law and library acquisition. *Nature* 220:922–23.

136. Goldhor, H., ed. 1968. *Research methods in librarianship: measurement and evaluation.* Champaign, Ill.: University of Illinois Bookstore.

137. Goodell, John S. 1975. *Libraries and work sampling.* Littleton, Colo.: Libraries Unlimited.

138. Gottschalk, C. M. 1970. System analysis considerations in decentralized international information systems. *ASIS proceedings* 9:211–13.

139. Goyal, S. K. 1973. Allocation of library funds to different departments of a university—an operational research approach. *College and research libraries* 34:219–22.

140. ————. 1970. Application of operational research to the

problem of determining appropriate loan periods for periodicals. *Libri* 20:94–100.

141. ———. 1972. A systematic method for reducing over ordering copies of books. *Library resources and technical services* 16:26–32.

142. Grose, Daphne. 1974. Some deprived information users. *ASLIB proceedings* 26:9–27.

143. Gull, C. D. 1968. Logical flow charts and other new techniques for the administration of libraries and information centers. *Library resources and technical services* 12:47–66.

144. Gupta, S. M., and Ravindran, A. 1974. Optimal storage of books by size: an operations research approach. *Journal of the American Society for Information Science* 25:354–57.

145. Haas, W. J. 1964. Description of a project to study the research library as an economic system. In *Association of Research Libraries, Minutes of the 63rd Meeting, January 26, 1964*. Chicago, Washington, D. C.: ARL.

146. Hamburg, M., Ramist, I. E. and Bommer, M. R. W. 1972. Library objectives and performance measures and their use in decision making. *Library quarterly* 42:107–28.

147. ———, et al. 1970. *Systems analysis of the library and information science data system: the research investigation, interim report to the U. S. Office of Education.* Philadelphia: University of Pennsylvania.

148. Hanson, C. W. 1953. How much space does a library need? *SIRA technical news* 9:60–64.

149. Hare, Van Court. 1967. *System analysis: a diagnostic approach.* New York: Harcourt.

150. Hawgood, J. 1967. Assessing the benefits of library innovations. In *Organization and handling of bibliographic records by computer.* New Castle Upon Tyne: Oriel Press.

151. Hayes, Robert M., and Becker, Joseph. 1974. *Handbook of data processing for libraries.* 2d. ed. Los Angeles: Melville.

152. Heiliger, Edward M., and Henderson, Paul B. 1971. *Library automation: experience, methodology and technology of the library as an information system.* New York: McGraw-Hill.

153. Heinritz, Fred J. 1973. Analysis and evaluation of current library procedures. *Library trends* 21:522–31.

154. ———. 1970. Quantitative management in libraries. *College and research libraries* 31:232–38.

155. Herner, Paul. 1967. Systems design, evaluation and costing. *Special libraries* 58:576–81.

156. Heyel, Carl. 1969. *Computers, office machines and the new information technology.* New York: Macmillan.

157. Hillier, J. 1962. Measuring the value of information services. *Journal of chemical documentation* 2:31–34.

158. Hindle, A. 1969. Models and measures for non-profit making services. In *Planning library services: proceedings of a research seminar, Lancaster, 1969.* University of Lancaster Library Occasional Papers, no. 3. Lancaster, England: University Library.

159. Hoadley, Irene B., and Clark, Alice, eds. 1972. *Quantitative methods in librarianship: standards, research management.* Proceedings and papers of the institute held at the Ohio State University, August 3–16, 1969. Westport, Conn.: Greenwood Press.

160. Hostrop, Richard W. 1973. *Managing education for results.* Homewood, Ill. ETC Publications.

161. Howard, Edward N. 1971. Toward PPBS in the public library. *American libraries* 2:386–93.

162. Hughes, John L. 1968. *Digital computer lab workbook.* Maynard, Mass.: Digital Equipment Corporation.

163. International Business Machines. 1963. *Basic system study guide.* White Plains, N.Y.

164. ———. 1971. *Decision tables, a systems analysis and documentation technique.* Data Processing Techniques Series. White Plains, N.Y.

165. ———. 1971. *Flowcharting techniques, data processing techniques.* White Plains, N.Y.

166. ———. 1972. *Library automation—introduction to data processing.* White Plains. N.Y.

167. ———. 1970. *Special academic computer concepts course for university, library and museum executives and scholarly associations in the humanities.* 2d ed. White Plains, N.Y.

168. Jahoda, G. 1974. Reference question analysis and search strategy development by man and machine. *Journal of the American Society for Information Science.* 25:139-44.

169. Jain, A. K. 1967. *Report on a statistical study of book use.* Library Operations Research Project. Lafayette, Ind.: Purdue University.

170. ———. 1972. Sampling in library book use. *Journal of the American Society for Information Science* 23:150-55.

171. ———, et al. 1969. A statistical model of book use and its application to the book storage problem. *Journal of the American Statistical Association.* 64:1211-24.

172. Jestes, Edward C. 1968. Example of systems analysis: locating a book in a reference room. *Special libraries* 59:722-28.

173. ———, and Laird, David W. 1968. A time study of general reference work in a university library. *Research in librarianship* 2:9-16.

174. Johnson, Richard A., et al. 1972. *Operations management: a systems concept.* New York: Houghton Mifflin.

175. Jones, Arthur. 1970. Criteria for the evaluation of public library service. *Journal of Librarianship* 2:228-45.

176. Jordan, John R. 1970. Let the computer select your reading list. *Datamation* 16:91-94.

177. Katz, Daniel, and Kahn, R. L. 1966. *The social psychology of organizations.* New York: Wiley.

178. Katzan, Harry, Jr. 1976. *Systems design and documentation: an introduction to the HIPO method.* New York: Van Nostrand Reinhold Co.

179. Kast, Fremont E., and Rosenzweig, James E. 1974. *Organization and management: a systems approach.* 2d ed. New York: McGraw-Hill.

180. Keller, J. E. 1969. Program budgeting and cost benefit

analysis in libraries. *College and research libraries* 30:156–60.

181. Kelly, William F. 1969. *Management through systems and procedures: the total systems concept.* New York: Wiley.

182. Kilgour, Frederick G. 1970. History of library computerization. *Journal of library automation* 3:218–29.

183. ———. 1967. Systems concepts and libraries. *College and research libraries* 28:167–70.

184. King, Donald, and Bryant, Edward. 1971. *The evaluation of information services and products.* Washington, D.C.

185. Klintoe, Kjeld. 1971. Cost analysis of a technical information unit. *ASLIB proceedings* 23:362–71.

186. Klir, G. J., ed. 1972. *Trends in general systems theory.* New York: Wiley.

187. Kohut, Joseph. 1974. Allocating the book budget: a model. *College and research libraries* 35:192–99.

188. Kountz, John C. 1968. Cost comparison of computer versus manual catalog maintenance. *Journal of library automation* 1:159–77.

189. ———. 1972. Library cost analysis: a recipe. *Library journal* 97:459–64.

190. Kozumplik, William A. 1967. Time and motion study of library operations. *Special libraries* 58:585–88.

191. Kraft, D. H., and McDonald, D. 1973. Library operations research: a tutorial. *Proceedings of the LARC Institute on Library Operations Research.* Washington, D.C.

192. Kuehl, Philip G. 1974. Marketing viewpoints for user need studies. In *Economics of information: a symposium,* ed. Robert S. Taylor, pp. 49–62. Syracuse University, School of Library Science.

193. Lamkin, Burton E. 1967. Systems analysis in top managment communication. *Special libraries* 58:90–94.

194. Lancaster, F. W. 1968. *Information retrieval systems: characteristics, testing and evaluation.* New York: Wiley.

195. ———, and Fayen, E. G. 1973. *Information retrieval: on-line.* Los Angeles: Melville.

196. Landau. Herbert. 1971. Can the librarian become a computer data bank manager? *Special libraries* 62:117-24.

197. LARC Association. 1971. *Are computer-oriented librarians really incompetent?* Tempe, Arizona: LARC.

198. Lazzaro, Victor, ed. 1968. *Systems and procedures: a handbook for business and industry.* Englewood Cliffs, N.J.: Prentice-Hall.

199. Leffler, W. L. 1964. A statistical method for circulation analysis. *College and research libraries* 25:488-90.

200. Leimkuhler, F. F., and Cox, J. G. 1964. Compact book storage in libraries. *Operations research* 12:419-27.

201. ———. 1973. Large scale library systems. *Library trends* 21:575-86.

202. ———. 1972. Library operations research: a process of discovery and justification. *Library trends* 42: 84-96.

203. ———. 1968. A literature search and file organization model. *American documentation* 19:131-36.

204. ———. 1967. *A literature search model.* Lafayette, Ind.: Purdue University.

205. ———. 1967. Mathematical models for library systems analysis. *Drexel Library quarterly* 4:185-96.

206. ———. 1969. On information storage models. In *Planning library services: proceedings of a research seminar, Lancaster, 1969.* University of Lancaster Library Occasional Papers, no. 3. Lancaster, England: University Library.

207. ———. 1973. Operations research and information science—a common cause. *ASIS journal* 24:29-32. ASIS Distinguished Lecture—1972.

208. ———. 1969. Storage policies for information systems. In *Planning library services: proceedings of a research seminar, Lancaster, 1969.* University of Lancaster Library Occassional Papers, no. 3. Lancaster, England: University Library.

209. ———. 1966. Systems analysis in university libraries. *College and research libraries* 27:13-18.

210. Line, M. B. 1973. The ability of a university library to

provide books wanted by researchers. *Journal of librarianship* 5:37-51.

211. Lipetz, B. A. 1970. *User requirements in identifying desired works in a large library.* New Haven, Conn.: Yale University Library.

212. Locke, William. 1970. Computer costs for large libraries. *Datamation* 16:69-74.

213. Lubans, J. 1971. Non-Use of academic library. *College and research libraries* 32:362-67.

214. Lubans, John R., Jr. and Chapman, Edward A., 1975. *Reader in library systems analysis.* Washington, D. C.: NCR Microcard.

215. Lucas, Henry R., Jr. 1974. Systems quality, user reactions and the use of information systems. *Management informatics* 3:207-12.

216. Luchsinger, Vincent P., and Dock, Thomas V. 1975. *The systems approach.* Dubuque, Iowa: Kendall/Hunt Publishing Company.

217. McDonald, D., and Craft, D. H. 1975. Library operations research: its past and our future. In *Accomplishment in information science,* ed. D. Hammer. Metuchen, N.J.: Scarecrow.

218. McGrawth, W. E. 1971. Correlating the subject of books taken out of and books used within an open stack library. *College and research libraries.* 32:280-85.

219. McInnes, R. M. 1972. The formula approach to library size: an empirical study of its efficiency in evaluating research libraries. *College and research libraries* 33:190-98.

220. Mackenzie, A. G. 1973. Systems analysis as a decision-making tool for the library manager. *Library trends* 21:493-504.

221. ———. 1968. Systems analysis of a university library. *Program* 2:7-14.

222. ——— and Stuart, I. M., eds. 1969. *Planning Library Services: Proceedings of a Research Seminar, Lancaster, 1969.* University of Lancaster Library Occasional Papers, no. 3. Lancaster, England: University Library.

223. Management Information Service. 1968. *Introduction to systems analysis.* Washington, D. C.: International City Manager's Association.
224. Markuson, Barbara E. 1970. An overview of library systems and automation programs. *Datamation* 16:60–68.
225. ———1966. Systems development study of the Library of Congress automation program. *Library quarterly* 36:197–233.
226. ——— et al. 1972. *Guidelines for library automation: a handbook for federal and other libraries.* Santa Monica, Calif.: Systems Development Corporation.
227. Marsterson, W. A. J. 1974. Users of libraries: a comparative study. *Journal of librarianship* 6:63–79.
228. Martin, Susan K., and Butler, Brett, eds. 1975. *Library automation: the state of the art II.* Papers presented at the Pre-Conference Institute on Library Automation held at Las Vegas, Nevada, June 22–23, 1973. Chicago: ALA.
229. Mason, Ellsworth. 1971. The great gas bubble prick't or computers revealed, a gentlemen of quality. *College and research libraries* 33:183–96.
230. Mather, Dan. 1968. Data processing in an academic library: some conclusions and observations. *PNLA quarterly* 32:14–21.
231. Matthews, A. 1970. Hurdles, problems, rewards: a total system concept at work. *American libraries* 1:151–53.
232. Maynard, H. B., ed. 1967. *Handbook of business administration.* New York: McGraw-Hill.
233. Meadow, Charles T. 1973. *The analysis of information systems.* 2d ed. Los Angeles: Melville.
234. Metcalf, K. D. 1955. Is it possible to pick the ideal size for large research libraries? In *International Congress of Libraries and Documentation Centres, Brussels, 1955, vol. 2A Communications.* La Haye: Nijhoff.
235. Millard, Patricia, comp. 1966. *Modern library equipment.* London: Crosby, Lockwood & Son.
236. Minder, Thomas. 1973. Application of systems analy-

sis in developing a new system. *Library trends* 21: 553-64.

237. ———. 1966. Library systems analyst: a job description. *College and research libraries* 27:271-76.

238. ———. 1968. *The regional library center in the mid-1970's; a concept paper.* Pittsburgh, Pa.: Graduate School of Library and Information Sciences.

239. Mlynarczyk, Frank, Jr. 1968. *Measuring library costs.* Presented at the Institute on Program Planning and Budgeting Systems for Libraries. Detroit: Wayne State University.

240. Moore, Edythe. 1967. Systems analysis: an overview. *Special libraries* 58:87-90.

241. Morelock, M., and Leimkuhler, F. F. 1964. Library operations research and systems engineering studies. *College and research libraries* 25:501-503.

242. Morris, Leslie R. 1972. Reclassification: flow-charting succeeds. *Catholic library world* 43:337-42.

243. Morse, P. M. 1968. *Library effectiveness: a systems approach.* Boston, Mass.: M.I.T.

244. ———. 1970. Search theory and browsing. *Library quarterly* 40:391-408.

245. ———. 1972. Measures of library effectiveness. *Library quarterly* 42:15-30.

246. ———. 1972. Optimal linear ordering of information items. *Operations research* 20:741-51.

247. ——— and Elston, C. 1969. A probabilistic model for obsolescence. *Operations research* 17:36-47.

248. Mostyn, Gregory R. 1974. The use of supply-demand equality in evaluating collection adequacy. *California libraries* 35:16-23.

249. Mott, Thomas H., Jr., Artandi, Susan, and Strunings, Leny. 1972. *Introduction to PL/1 programming for library and information science.* New York: Academic Press.

250. Myers, Rose. 1972. Library self evaluation. In *Quantitative Methods in librarianship,* eds. Irene Braden and Alice S. Clark, pp. 61-65. Westport, Conn.: Greenwood Press.

251. Nance, R. E. 1970. An analytical model of a library network. *ASIS journal* 23:237-47.
252. ———— and Baker, N. R. 1971. Library policy structure: an industrial dynamics study. *Simulation* 17:109-23
253. National Microfilm Association. 1973. *Introduction to micrographics.* Silver Spring, Maryland: NMA.
254. Neelameghan, A. 1972. Systems approach in the study of the attributes of the universe of subjects. *Library science with a slant towards documentation* 9:445-72.
255. Nelson, J. B. 1972. *Work measurement.* Blacksburg, Virginia: Virginia Polytechnic Institute and State University.
256. Nie, Norman, et al. 1975. *SPSS: statistical package for the social sciences.* 2nd ed. New York: McGraw-Hill.
257. Oh, T. K. 1966. New dimensions of management theory. *College and research libraries* 27:431-38.
258. Olson, E. E., Liesener, J. W. and Craft, D. H. 1972. An educational model for library problem solving: teaming librarians, students and faculty. *Special libraries* 63:231-34.
259. O'Neill, E. T. 1966. Sampling university library collections. *College and research libraries* 27:450-54.
260. Orr, R. H. 1973. Measuring the goodness of library services: a general framework for considering quantitative measures. *Journal of documentation* 29:315-33.
261. Optner, Stanford L. 1975. *Systems analysis for business management.* 3d ed. Englewood Cliffs, N.J.: Prentice-Hall.
262. Palmer, F. M. 1968. Computer programming for the librarian. *Drexel library quarterly* 4:197-213.
263. Palmer, R. P. 1973. *Case studies in library computer systems.* New York: Bowker.
264. Patrinostra, Frank S., et al. 1973. *Available data banks for library and information services.* Tempe, Arizona: Library Automation and Consulting Association (LARC).
265. Penner, R. J. 1972. Measuring a library's capability. *Journal of education for librarianship* 13:17-30.

266. Pfiffner, John M., and Lane, Owen S. 1964. *Manual for administrative analysis.* Los Angeles: University of Southern California.

267. Pings, Vern M. 1968. Development of quantitative assessment of medical libraries. *College and research libraries* 29:373-80.

268. Pitt, W. B., Kraft, D. H. and Heilprin, L. B. 1974. Buy or copy? A library operations research model. Paper presented at the 20th International Meeting of the Institute of Management Sciences, Tel Aviv, Israel, June 1973. *Information storage and retrieval* 10:331-41.

269. Poage, S. T. 1960. Sampling in library administration. *Library quarterly* 30:213-18.

270. Pratt, Allan D. 1969. Flow charting. In *Library use of computers: an introduction,* eds. Gloria L. Smith and Robert S. Meyer. New York: Special Libraries Association.

271. Price, D. J. De Solla. 1963. *Little science, big science.* New York: Columbia University Press.

272. Price, D. S. 1974. The cost of information: a prerequisite for other analysis. In *Economics of information dissemination, a symposium,* ed. Robert S. Taylor. Syracuse, New York: Syracuse University, School of Library Science.

273. Pritchard, Alan. 1973. *The library as an industrial firm: an approach to library management.* London: City of London Polytechnic Library and Learning Resources Services.

274. ———, and Auckland, Mary. 1973. *Book ordering and processing system study.* London: City of London Polytechnic Library and Learning Resources Service.

275. Raffel, Jeffrey A. 1974. From economic to political analysis of library decision making. *College and research libraries* 35:412-23.

276. ———, and Shisko, R. 1969. *Systematic analysis of university libraries: an application of cost-benefit analysis to the M.I.T. libraries.* Cambridge, Mass.: M.I.T.

277. Raisig, L. M. 1960. Mathematical evaluation of the scientific serial. *Science* 131:1417-19.
278. Ratcliffe, F. W. 1970. Manchester University Library Bindery: a study of library efficiency and management. *Libri* 20:77-88.
279. Redmond, D. A. 1966. Optimum size: the special library viewpoint. *Sci-Tech news* 20:40-42.
280. Reisman, A., et al. 1972. Timeliness of library materials delivery: a set of priorities. *Socio-economic planning sciences* 6:145-52.
281. Robinson, F., et al. 1969. *Symplegades: systems analysis in libraries*. New Castle Upon Tyne, England: Oriel Press.
282. Rosen, Saul. 1969. Electronic computers: a historical survey. *Computing surveys* 1:7-36.
283. Rosenberg, K. C. 1969. Evaluation of an industrial library, a simple minded technique. *Special libraries* 60:635-38.
284. Ross, J., and Brooks, J. 1972. Costing manual and computerized library circulation systems. *Program* 6:217-27.
285. Rothery, Brian, ed. 1971. *The art of systems analysis*. Englewood Cliffs, N.J.: Prentice-Hall.
286. Rouse, W. B., ed. 1973. *Applications of operations research techniques in Tufts University libraries*. Medford, Mass.: College of Engineering, Tufts University.
287. ———, and Rouse, S. H. 1973. Use of a librarian/consultant team to study library operation. *College and research libraries* 34:242-48.
288. Ruecking, F. 1964. Selecting a circulation-control system: A mathematical approach. *College and research libraries* 25:385-90.
289. Rzasa, Philip V., and Baker, Norman R. 1972. Measures of effectiveness for a university library. *Journal of the American Society for Information Science* 23:248-53.
290. Salton, Gerard. 1975. *Dynamic information and library processing*. Englewood Cliffs, N.J.: Prentice-Hall.

291. Salverson, Carol A. 1969. The relevance of statistics to library evaluation. *College and research libraries* 30:352-62.

292. Saracevic, T., ed. 1970. *Introduction to information science.* New York: Bowker.

293. Schneider, John H., et al. eds. 1973. *Survey of commercially available computer-readable bibliographic data bases.* Washington, D. C.: American Society for Information Science.

294. Schultheiss, John. 1966. Systems analysis and planning. In *Data Processing in public and university libraries,* ed. John Harvey. Washington, D. C.: Spartan Books.

295. Sewell, P.H . 1968. The evaluation of library services in depth. *UNESCO bulletin for libraries* 22:274-80.

296. Simms, Daniel M. 1968. What is a system analyst? *Special libraries* 59:718-21.

297. Singh, Jagjit. 1972. *Great ideas of operational research.* New York: Dover.

298. Slater, F., ed. 1973. *Cost reduction for special libraries.* Washington, D. C.: American Society for Information Science.

299. Smith, Gloria L., and Meyer, Robert S. 1969. *Library use of computers: an introduction.* New York: Special Libraries Association.

300. Standera, Oldrich R. 1974. Costs and effectiveness in the evolution of an information system: a case study. *ASIS journal* 25:203-207.

301. Stevenson, C. C. 1967. Checklist for review and evaluation of technical libraries. *Special libraries* 58:106-10.

302. Swanson, Rowena Weiss. 1974. *Systems analysis + work study = accountability.* Colorado: Southeast Metropolitan Board of Cooperative Service.

303. Swenson, Sally. 1965. Flowchart on library searching techniques. *Special libraries* 56:239-42.

304. Thomas, P. A. 1971. *Task analysis of library operations.* ASLIB Occasional Publication, no. 8. London: ASLIB.

305. ———and East H., 1968. Comments on the terminology

of the analysis of library systems and the functions of forms therein. *ASLIB proceedings* 20:340-44.

306. ———and Robertson, S. E. 1975. Computer simulation model of library operations. *Journal of documentation* 31:1-18.

307. Trueswell, R. W. 1969. Some behavioral patterns of library users: the 80/20 Rule. *Wilson Library bulletin* 43:458-61.

308. ———. 1969. User circulation satisfaction vs. size of holdings at three academic libraries. *College and research libraries* 30:204-13.

309. U.S. Atomic Energy Commission, Division of Technical Information. 1968. *Computers*. Oak Ridge, Tenn.

310. U.S. Dept. of the Army. 1967. *Techniques of work simplification*. U.S. Dept. of the Army Pamphlet 1-52. Washington, D.C.: Government Printing Office.

311. Urquhart, J. A., and Schofield, J. L. 1971. Measuring reader's failure at the shelf. *Journal of documentation* 27:273-86.

312. Van, Amerongen C. 1974. *The way things work, book of the computer: an illustrated encyclopedia of information science, cybernetics and data processing*. New York: Simon and Schuster.

313. Van Gigch, John P. 1974. *Applied general systems theory*. New York: Harper and Row.

314. Vaughn, William J., and Dunn, J. D. 1974. A study of job satisfaction in six university libraries. *College and research libraries* 35: 163-77.

315. Veaner, Allen B. 1970. Major decision points in library automation. *College and research libraries* 31:299-312.

316. ———. 1971. Approaches to library automation. *Law library journal* 64:146-53.

317. Vickery, B. C. 1969. Indicators of the use of periodicals. *Journal of librarianship* 1:170-82.

318. Wallace, W. Lyle, ed. 1962. *Work simplification*. Systems Education Monograph, no. 1. Detroit, Mich.: Systems and Procedures Association.

319. Warheit, I. A. 1971. When some library systems fail—is

it the system or the librarian? *Wilson Library bulletin* 46:52–58.

320. Wasserman, P. 1958. Measuring performance in a special library—problems and prospects. *Special libraries* 49:377–82.

321. Weber, D. C. 1957. Criteria for evaluating a college library. *Association of American Colleges bulletin* 43:629–35.

322. Weinberg, C. B. 1974. The university library: analysis and proposals. *Management Science* 21:130–40.

323. Weisman, Herman M. 1972. *Information systems, services, and centers.* New York: Wiley Becker-Hayes.

324. Wessel, C. J. 1968. Criteria for evaluating technical library effectiveness. *ASLIB proceedings* 20:455–81.

325. Whitehall, T. 1967. Time to think: use of the systems approach to the problems of the one-man information unit. *ASLIB proceedings* 19:406–15.

326. Whitehead, Clay T. 1967. *Uses and limitations of systems analysis.* Santa Monica, Calif.: Rand Corporation.

327. Whittemore, Bruce J., and Yovits, Marshall C. 1974. The quantification and analysis of information used in decision process. *Information science* 7:171–84.

328. Wiener, Norbert. 1954. *The human use of human beings: cybernetics and society.* New York: Doubleday.

329. Williams, B. J. 1966. Work simplification techniques in libraries. *South Carolina librarian* 11:9–11.

330. Williams G., et al. 1968. *Library cost models: owning versus borrowing serial publications, report.* Chicago: Center for Research libraries.

331. Wilson, John H., Jr. 1972. Costs, budgeting and economics of information processing. In *Annual review of information science and technology,* vol. 7, pp. 39–67. Washington, D.C.: American Society for Information Science.

332. Woodruff, Elaine. 1957. Work measurement applied to libraries. *Special libraries* 48:139–44.

333. Wood, D. N. 1969. Discovering the user and his information needs. *ASLIB proceedings* 21:262-70.
334. ———1971. User studies: a review of the literature from 1960 to 1970. *ASLIB proceedings* 23:11-23.
335. Woodburn, I. A. 1969. Mathematical model of a hierarchial library system. In *Planning library services: proceedings of a research seminar, Lancaster, 1969.* University of Lancaster Library Occasional Paper, no. 3. Lancaster, England: University Library.
336. Yourdon, Edward, and Constantine, Larry L. 1975. *Structured design.* New York: Yourdon, Inc.

Question and Exercise Index

General Index